BUILDING COMMITMENT TO
REFORM

THROUGH STRATEGIC COMMUNICATION

Building Commitment to Reform through Strategic Communication: The Five Key Decisions is available as an interactive textbook at http://www.worldbank.org/pdt. The interactive textbook allows reform managers and their teams, communities of practice, and colleagues working in sectors and regions, as well as students and teachers, to share notes and related materials for an enhanced multimedia learning and knowledge-exchange experience.

Further, an interactive decision tool on Five Key Decisions is available as ancillary material, to help teams apply strategic communication concepts to programs, projects, and policy reform through case examples and quizzes. The decision tool can be accessed at an external Web site (http://www.worldbank.org/commgap) or at an internal World Bank Web site available to Bank staff worldwide (http://hrslo).

BUILDING COMMITMENT TO REFORM

THROUGH STRATEGIC COMMUNICATION

The Five Key Decisions

CECILIA CABAÑERO-VERZOSA
AND
HELEN R. GARCIA

THE WORLD BANK
Washington, DC

1818 H Street NW
Washington DC 20433
Telephone: 202-473-1000
Internet: www.worldbank.org
E-mail: feedback@worldbank.org

ISBN: 978-0-8213-7621-8
eISBN: 978-0-8213-7622-5
DOI: 10.1596/978-0-8213-7621-8

Library of Congress cataloging-in-publication data has been applied for

Cover: Naylor Design, Inc.
Editing and composition: UpperCase Publication Services, Ltd.

Contents

Boxes

Figures

Tables

Acknowledgments

This workbook has been the product of many years of work with senior government officials in developing countries around the world, with World Bank colleagues, as well as with partners in donor agencies and international development organizations. The management decision tool offered to readers in this volume has been discussed, tested, applied, and adapted by many practitioners. By offering examples from sectors and regions, we hope to demonstrate how this decision tool can provide reform managers and their teams with a systematic and practical approach that is grounded in communication and behavioral science theory.

We would like to thank some 8,000 people worldwide who participated in strategic communication courses delivered by the World Bank and its institutional partners. The courses were delivered in classrooms and through distance learning modalities, including e-learning sessions with online facilitation and computer-based, self-paced instructional modules. This decision tool has been a centerpiece of these strategic communication courses and learning interventions. We hope this workbook will deepen the appreciation of the valuable role that strategic communication plays in building and sustaining support for reform.

To illustrate how the five key decisions shaped the communication strategy in projects, programs, and policy reform, we worked with key individuals who led reform efforts or played strategic roles in designing interventions. They helped us describe their communication strategies and assess how these have contributed to the success of reform. We thank these individuals for their collaboration on the illustrative cases: Benjamin Herzberg (investment climate reform in Bosnia and Herzegovina); Sina Odugbemi and Masud Mozammel (Moldova's poverty reduction strategy);

Daniel Cotlear (accountability in social reform in Peru); Leonora Aquino-Gonzales (the country assistance strategy for the Philippines); Jose Edgardo L. Campos, Ruby Alvarez, Cecilia D. Vales, and Leonora Aquino-Gonzales (public procurement reform in the Philippines); and Paul D. Mitchell (the West African Gas Pipeline).

We also thank several institutional partners who have codelivered many courses with us: the Academy for Educational Development (Ann Jimerson, Brian McCotter, Stephanie McNulty, Mark Rasmuson, Rose Mary Romano, Anton Schneider, William A. Smith, and John Strand); Harvard University Kennedy School of Government (Gary Orren); Chlopak, Leonard, and Schechter, CLS (Peter Schechter); CM Partners (Gardner Heaton, Stacy Heen, Eric Henry, and Tom Schaub); Georgetown University (Alan R. Andreasen); University of Minnesota Hubert Humphrey School of Public Affairs (Thomas R. Fiutak); the United States Centers for Disease Control and the University of Georgia (Vicki Freimuth); the Communication Center (Tom Hoag, Susan Peterson, Nathan Roberts, and Shelley Sims); the Asian Institute of Management, the Philippines (Eduardo L. Roberto and Francisco Roman); Wells Advertising, the Philippines (Jose Rafael Hernandez); and TRENDS, the Philippines (Mercy Abad).

We appreciate the guidance and financial support of the World Bank's Human Resources Leadership for Organizational Effectiveness team and the World Bank's Knowledge and Learning Board, which enabled us to deliver these learning programs to World Bank staff and to the World Bank Institute for learning interventions offered to senior government officials and their project teams. Thanks to our colleagues at External Affairs who have helped to make this publication possible: Paul D. Mitchell, Umou S. Al-Bazzaz, and the Office of the Publisher (Carlos E. Rossel, Santiago Pombo-Bejarano, Nancy Lammers, Rick Ludwick, Andrés Meneses, and Patricia Katayama).

About the Authors

Cecilia Cabañero-Verzosa is communication advisor at the World Bank Institute's Governance Practice. She has extensive experience in the design and management of communication interventions for reform across sectors and regions, with recent work in governance and anticorruption programs. She created the Strategic Communication Learning Program at the World Bank—a program that has reached some 8,000 participants, including World Bank managers, sector specialists, project teams and their developing-country partners, and communication specialists. She delivered learning programs in various formats—from classroom sessions to e-learning modules, videotaped simulations, and online performance support tools. Before joining the World Bank, she worked with two international organizations, served as executive director of a civil society organization working on social marketing in health, and provided technical support on strategic communication to developing-country programs worldwide.

Helen Garcia is a World Bank consultant working in the Communication for Governance and Accountability Program (CommGAP), External Affairs Vice Presidency (EXT). She has been involved in CommGAP's program on research and advocacy, as well as in training and capacity building. Prior to this, she was involved in economic and sector work focusing on poverty and social development issues in Africa, Asia, Eastern Europe, Latin America, and the Middle East. She served the Bank's Executive Board as a staff member in the Executive Director's Office, where she provided advisory and technical support. Before joining the World Bank, Garcia was part of a major research project on food security and poverty in the International Food Policy Research Institute. In the Philippines, she served the government as director for social development in the Office of the Prime Minister, and as director for policy research in the National Council on Integrated Area Development.

Abbreviations

CAS	country assistance strategy
CPAR	Country Procurement Assessment Report
EGPRSP	Economic Growth and Poverty Reduction Strategy Paper
GDP	gross domestic product
GPPB	Government Procurement Policy Board
KDC	Knowledge for Development Center
LGU	local government unit
NGO	nongovernmental organization
OED	Operations Evaluation Department
PRSP	Poverty Reduction Strategy Paper
RECURSO	Rendición de Cuentas para la Reforma Social; Accountability in Social Reform
TWG	technical working group
WAGP	West African Gas Pipeline [Project]
WAPCo	West African Gas Pipeline Company

All dollar amounts are U.S. dollars, unless otherwise indicated.

Introduction

Development practitioners long have known that successful reforms typically are those that have the strong support of key stakeholders and that are understood by the general public. Increased stakeholder engagement in development and reform interventions enables people to acquire the new knowledge that will shape their attitudes and prompt them to adopt the positive behaviors that affect evolving social norms. And they realize that a communication strategy thoughtfully designed to connect with key audiences is the way to increase their stakeholders' levels of engagement and their commitment to sustained development and needed reform. They have seen growing evidence that communication is critical to generating broad support for reforms, but they can find few materials that outline a pragmatic, concise, and rigorously tested approach to using strategic communication to support reform efforts. All of that is why we have created this workbook.

Although program managers, policy makers, and reform leaders bear responsibility for integrating communication activities with the design of reform and program interventions, they may have limited professional training and experience in the art and science of communication. This workbook has been written primarily for those people interested in learning to use *strategic communication* to build broad-based commitment to reform.

In the development and reform context, "strategic communication" refers to the design of action plans intended to promote voluntary changes in behavior among stakeholders whose endorsements are critical to a reform initiative's success. These action plans become instruments of policy and program reform, not merely a schedule for distributing information. Strategic communication employs the tools of persuasion and negotiation—rather than the power of laws, coercion, or incentives—to identify involved parties' underlying interests and promote their understanding of and support for a proposed reform.

The goal of strategic communication is to change behavior, to prompt people to do something in a manner that differs from how they are doing it when the communication effort begins. The change may be intended for individuals, groups of people within an organization, a mass of communities within a society, or an entire nation. In this workbook, "behavior change" also encompasses a corollary change in beliefs and the adoption of new attitudes, which then increase the likelihood that a person will change his or her behavior. New beliefs, attitudes, and behaviors adopted by large cohorts of people in a given society shape that society's social norms.

Strategic communication begins with two assumptions: (1) the status quo is not adequate and (2) change is necessary. Thus, it raises the ante for communication. By seeking change as its ultimate goal, it goes beyond the traditional approach whereby reform managers used communication simply to generate awareness of an issue, to educate the public about the need for reform to address that issue, and to persuade people that a proposed reform will benefit them. Those people who use strategic communication understand that where communication is not used to help people voluntarily adopt the type of change that will produce and sustain a reform, its full power has not been tapped.

We begin with two beliefs: (1) managers, project teams, reform leaders, and policy makers appreciate the value of communication in achieving reform; and (2) they are seeking a systematic approach to develop a communication strategy that changes what people know, believe in, and do so that their reforms have a better chance of success. Therefore, we pose decisions that managers must make to formulate a communication strategy that will support and sustain their development interventions.

Development organizations use communication tools and approaches to serve their objectives in a number of ways. Mefalopulos (2008) identifies four types of communication used by these organizations: corporate, internal, advocacy, and development. *Corporate communication* promotes the organization's mission, explains its programs, and creates a brand and a position for the organization in the minds of its constituencies and clients. *Internal communication,* which may be part of corporate communication, refers to the flow of information between management and staff concerning organizational policies and practices. It aims to promote the cohesive organizational culture needed to conduct the organization's business effectively. *Advocacy communication* articulates the organization's stance on development issues and facilitates dialogue on critical development challenges. *Development communication* endeavors to enhance the effectiveness of development policies, programs, and projects by engaging stakeholders throughout the design, implementation, and monitoring of these interventions.

Why a Workbook on Strategic Communication?

This workbook gives the reader a management decision-making tool for developing a communication strategy that will support a proposed reform. This decision tool helps a reform project team focus its efforts by disciplining it to select only those communication activities that will prompt its target audiences to learn new information and adopt positive attitudes that lead to desired changes in behavior. The decision-making approach described here also helps program managers work more effectively with communication specialists. This tool has been used by program managers in developing countries and taught at workshops and in formal courses conducted face-to-face; by videoconference; and through self-paced, computer-based modules. To illustrate how this tool may be used in various types of development activities and in diverse settings, we provide examples drawn from projects, economic and sector work, country assistance strategies formulated by donor groups, and country programs designed by developing-country government teams to reduce poverty.

How to Use This Workbook

The material here is organized to help managers prepare a communication strategy as they reach decisions about existing policy issues and about the options they have for policy reform and development initiatives. Program managers may use this workbook to integrate strategic communication in their thinking about the nature of reform interventions in either or both of the following ways:

1. When there is little time and resources are limited, use the Five Communication Management Decision tool (chapter 1) to guide discussions in a team meeting. These five decisions are described briefly and accompanied by a set of questions for team discussions.
2. When issues are complex, take the time to refer to the examples of effective use of strategic communication provided in chapters 2 through 8. Discover how various types of reforms have used communication to create understanding of and build support for reform goals. Involve a communication specialist in the early stages of designing the reform program. Use the tool to brief the communication specialist on the potential role of strategic communication in promoting reform goals.

The decision tool illustrated and explained in chapter 1 is completed and presented in each of the example chapters.

In each country case, the decision tool summarizes the communication strategy that guided communication activities. The tool enables reform managers and their teams to have an overall perspective of reform goals and how communication approaches can be used to create understanding of, and build support for, reform. It helps teams decide which communication activities are strategic and which may have peripheral value, enabling them to make best use of scarce communication resources.

Reference

Mefalopulos, Paolo. 2008. *Development Communication Sourcebook: Broadening the Boundaries of Communication.* Washington, DC: World Bank.

1

Using Strategic Communication to Build Commitment to Reform

Strategic communication is a stakeholder- or client-centered approach to promote voluntary changes in people's knowledge, attitudes, and behaviors to achieve development objectives. In employing strategic communication, reform managers seek to understand the stakeholder's or client's perspective on proposed development interventions or on a given policy recommendation, rather than merely promoting their organization's position on this development issue. Strategic communication helps managers be more focused on the stakeholder or client than on the organization in their communication efforts.[1]

Also loosely labeled "public sector marketing," "social marketing," and "behavior change communication," strategic communication is "designed to advance particular policies or organizational strategies by making them comprehensible and by enlisting the support and cooperation of those who must work together to produce the intended result" (Moore 1995).

Furthermore, strategic communication raises the ante for communication—which goes beyond raising awareness to using communication to assist stakeholders or clients in learning new information and developing new attitudes to facilitate adoption of new behaviors. The program's development objectives are achieved when large groups of people voluntarily have changed behaviors in ways that lead to targeted development results. For example, if the project goal is to improve girls' education, the increased rate of secondary-school-age girls completing secondary school and receiving a high-quality education implies that parents have provided the means to have their daughters complete secondary school and that school teachers and administrators have provided high-quality education. Therefore, communication activities would have addressed the communication needs of multiple audiences—parents, teachers, school administrators, government officials—to enable those groups to acquire new knowledge, develop more positive attitudes about the benefits of having girls complete secondary school, and adopt improved practices that complement behavior change efforts of other relevant groups, ultimately resulting in the achievement of project goals.

A *communication strategy* consists of management decisions that guide the communication plan itself. A communication strategy identifies people whose support is critical to the success of reform, the type of behaviors that need to be adopted by various groups to help achieve project objectives, messages that will resonate with relevant audiences, channels of communication that will reach people and be credible, and measures of communication effectiveness (see figure 1.1).

Whereas a communication strategy provides the overall framework and set of management decisions to guide communication activities, a communication plan provides an implementation timeline and budget, and it describes specific communication activities that need to be undertaken.

How can strategic communication help reforms succeed? It plays a key role at various stages, whether the reforms are conducted at the national or international level; or whether they are directed at promoting societal change, institutional change, or change associated with specific program goals and policy reform efforts. In the beginning of the change process, leaders may use strategic communication to explain the rationale behind an intended change, and thus engage people in a consultative effort to better understand the nature of the problem that is prompting the adoption of new programs or policies. When

Figure 1.1. Elements of Strategic Communication

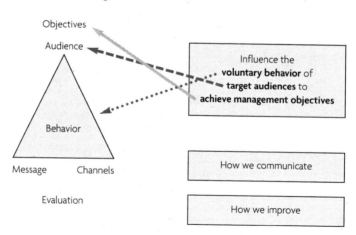

Source: World Bank Strategic Communication Knowledge and Learning Program, 2008.

launched, change initiatives must be understood by a broad array of audiences. Developing support for reform often requires that leaders encourage people to revise their thinking, their attitudes, and their practices. Asking for such profound change demands a style of communication that will engage the audience, prompt its buying into the proposed reform, and move it to action. When the new interventions have been under way for a while, with critical milestones reached and key goals achieved, sustaining its success requires that policy makers and program managers continually respond to stakeholders' and clients' concerns, reduce barriers to the adoption of new practices, and tap into evolving social norms to encourage people to maintain positive behaviors.

Reforms need time to take root, and reformers need to use strategic communication to build stakeholders' commitment over the long haul. Communicating proof of successes realized and difficulties encountered during periods of reform and engaging stakeholders in continuous problem-solving and option-building activities are communication tasks that build the basis for desired reform outcomes. Stakeholders who are crucial to the success of a specific reform also may change their own beliefs and actions. As they gain new knowledge, stakeholders may change their views on policy and program priorities, may switch allegiances to political parties, and may align with different interest groups. The communication strategy needed in the early stages of a reform, when passing enabling legislation may be the primary concern, differs from the communication strategy needed to implement a policy reform when the laws have been passed. Communication strategy must be grounded in the current reality, while considering the past and anticipating future scenarios.

Strategic Communication Is a Management Decision

The success of strategic communication does not depend on creative messages or enticing incentives to try new practices. Rather, it demands a clear understanding of the perceptions, motivations, beliefs, and practices of everyone involved in or affected by a reform program. Change cannot be effective unless decisions about policy or program interventions are based on that understanding.

Communication research provides the lens through which program managers can understand people's perspectives on proposed reforms. Research can uncover people's lack of information or misinformation about the prevalence or importance of a development problem. It can provide managers with a deeper understanding of why people behave the way they do, which may go against what technocrats consider ideal practices that will lead to the achievement of development results.[2] When an effective communication strategy is not considered in the early planning stages of a reform initiative—when it is instead an afterthought used mainly as a means to disseminate information—managers jeopardize the potential long-term success of the planned reform. In its rightful place as the first step in a reform effort, designing a communication strategy makes it imperative that reform agents begin by viewing the reform through the eyes of those who are going to be affected by reform measures, whether positively or negatively. Only when communication is an integral part of the manager's decision-making process in analyzing a development problem and identifying solutions does communication become strategic. Because the support and active involvement of stakeholders, clients, and audiences will be critical to the success of any reform process, strategic communication suited to those stakeholders, clients, and audiences should guide the manager's thinking about what solutions might be feasible.

When the goal of communication is beyond merely informing the general public about reforms—when it is meant to create an environment that encourages behavioral change in support of a reform's success—the reform leaders must take responsibility for crafting and delivering communication that is effective in both form and content.

Communication is no longer the exclusive purview of communication specialists, public relations practitioners, political consultants, or strategy advisers. In matters of reform, it becomes part of the design and implementation process, engaging constituencies in constructive dialogue and promoting participation in public scrutiny and debate. Reform managers will need to direct and guide the communication effort. They also need to engage multiple stakeholders, clients, and audiences in dialogue and debate so as to anticipate stakeholder needs and concerns. In undertaking these communication tasks, it will be ideal if they are able to obtain the technical support of communication specialists, whether from their own organizations or from academia, the private sector, or civil society organizations.

Anchor a Reform's Communication Strategy on Its Management Objectives

Management objectives describe the development problem that a specific reform seeks to address. Managers define these in terms of the development problem and the desired outcome of reform efforts. Management objectives articulate the nature of reform, its rationale, and the development outcomes sought. It is useful to articulate management objectives at an appropriate level; typically, management objectives (often referred to by development practitioners as "project development objectives" in the logical framework of a project) are written in broad general statements.

A communication objective describes how communication concepts, approaches, and tools will be used to achieve the management objectives. Thus, the ultimate communication objective will be to increase adoption of new behaviors by critical stakeholders, clients, and audiences so that the management objectives are achieved. By distinguishing the management objective from a communication objective, managers gain a clearer view of the communication task (which is to provide information, create persuasive messages, and develop arenas for dialogue and engagement). Communication activities aim to help stakeholders gain new knowledge and acquire more positive attitudes toward the development intervention, thus facilitating voluntary changes in behavior. Managers will need to realize that communication is one element of the development intervention, albeit a critical and often overlooked aspect of the design and implementation of change processes inherent in development work. For example, a nationwide communication campaign to increase immunizations may persuade families with young children to take their children to health facilities in a timely manner. But if health workers do not have vaccines on hand, are not trained adequately to provide immunizations, or do not practice good client engagement skills at the health center, the immunization program is doomed to fail. Communication must go hand in hand with quality services or, in the case of policy reforms, with politically feasible policy options.

Communication strategy supports the attainment of a reform's management objectives in at least three ways: (1) by increasing awareness and knowledge about the problem being addressed by the reform; (2) by promoting a positive change in people's beliefs, attitudes, and behaviors; and (3) by encouraging the adoption of new practices that help the reform succeed. Although employing communication to generate awareness of a development issue or to create positive attitudes about reform is useful, it falls short of what is needed to help reform succeed over the long term. Ultimately, strategic communication should be used to promote behavioral and practical change because reform initiatives will succeed only when large groups of people are ready to take positive action and embrace new practices. Managers must anchor their communication approaches on the intended reform outcomes—their management objectives—and wed them with services that enable people to adopt the new practices that constitute successful reform.

Act to Avoid Common Pitfalls

Both reform leaders and communication specialists may encounter difficulties in using communication to facilitate changes in knowledge, attitudes, and practices. Knowing how communication may be misused, underused, or poorly understood can help you avoid those difficulties. Here is some advice for avoiding or addressing problems:

1. Determine when communication activities are "off strategy." A carefully conceived communication strategy is a road map that policy makers and reform agents use to judge whether specific communication activities are helping achieve a specific management objective or are out of line with the established strategy. Managers often think of communication in terms of its physical elements—print materials, press releases, media spots, and road shows—rather than assessing whether those elements actually contribute to

achieving management objectives. Activities or outputs that have no direct relevance to the objectives are off strategy and should be discontinued because they waste scarce resources.

2. Push the envelope—promote awareness that leads to action, not just to knowledge. There are specific types of information that help people adopt new behavior: information that helps them judge whether adopting a new behavior will benefit rather than disadvantage them, information on social norms that identifies other credible authorities who consider the new behavior valuable, and information that helps people visualize what it will take to adopt a new behavior and realize that the steps are within their control and ability to execute.

3. Keep your strategy flexible and responsive to changes in the reform environment. A successful communication strategy is inspiring, creative, interactive, and ever-changing. It should be grounded firmly in an understanding of people's perceptions (or misperceptions), their attitudes about a given reform, and their assessment of whether new practices are feasible in the context of their daily lives. People constantly are bombarded with new information, and they may reject it or become motivated to try new practices. Periodically review the communication strategy designed to support the reform and realign communication management decisions with changes in people's knowledge, attitudes, and behaviors.

4. Remember that audiences dictate strategy and organizations execute strategy. A communication strategy centered on the audience's needs, perceptions, and motivations has a greater probability of success than does one based primarily on an organization's goals and ambitions. Organizations providing services and information that people care about are more likely to succeed in achieving their organizational goals because their messages are in sync with the products and services they offer. Both the organization's communication and its products and services respond to what people need or want rather than to what the organization would like to "sell" or promote. Organizations that devise communication strategies by looking first at their own mission and development issues without gaining a deep understanding of their audiences' perceptions of those same issues are creating one-way communication: they are advocating for reform while their audiences and intended beneficiaries have little awareness of why the reform is needed and how it might affect their lives.

5. Articulate the management objective(s) before developing a communication strategy to support and realize it. When a management objective is unclear, the communication strategy is sure to fail. When a management objective is complex or when there are several objectives, subdivide and prioritize the objectives that will benefit from intensive communication support. "Unpacking" objectives enables planners to design specific communication strategies to support each one.

In a forestry project in Latin America, the project team stated its management objective as "reducing deforestation." When a management objective is stated so broadly, it is difficult to determine which behaviors should be changed among what audiences to achieve the reform's objective. To unpack that broad management objective, the team needed to ask these questions: What causes deforestation? What are people doing or not doing? And why? The project team discovered that farmers who were burning large tracts of forestland to make the land usable for agriculture were causing the deforestation. The team reformulated its management objective as "reducing the destruction of forests by farmers" and thus realized that it was the farmers' behavior that needed to change. The primary audience for the reform's communication strategy consisted of farmers living near forested lands, and the behavior change goal was to discourage the burning of forest areas for agriculture. The communication objectives, therefore, were (1) to increase knowledge about the dire consequences of deforestation; (2) to influence adoption of positive attitudes toward conserving forest areas, while persuading farmers that there were alternative ways to earn a livelihood from farming without resorting to massive burning of forest areas; (3) to show farmers how others have been successful in earning a decent livelihood from agriculture without burning forestlands; and (4) to help farmers voluntarily decide to change their practices and to adopt new behaviors.

That example reveals how strategic communication contributes to achieving management objectives—not by disseminating information but by viewing reform goals from the perspectives of audiences and stakeholders and then establishing communication objectives that address those perspectives. The communication activities then are designed to bring about changes in knowledge, attitudes, and behaviors among people whose current behaviors have contributed to the problem that a reform is seeking to address.

The Five Communication Management Decisions

A communication strategy articulates, explains, and promotes a vision and a set of carefully considered project development objectives. It creates a consistent, unified "voice" that links diverse activities and goals in a way that appeals to stakeholders and audiences. The strategy is established before decisions are made on tactics—the concrete steps to be taken and the techniques to be used in realizing communication goals.

In this section, we offer a practical approach to developing a communication strategy to support reforms, basing the strategy on five core decisions. Before managers approach these five decisions, however, they must define the management objective clearly because their subsequent communication strategy decisions must support the overall management objective.

Development reform objectives are based on the assumption that problematic conditions are hindering development and need to be changed. An articulated management objective describes what policy makers and reform agents expect to achieve if the reforms succeed. But to be meaningful in creating a communication strategy, the management objective also needs to be stated in a way that defines the cause of the current problem and the practices that contribute to the problem. Communication then may be designed not only to increase awareness about the general problem, but also to promote changes in knowledge, attitudes, and behaviors that will contribute to the achievement of objectives and the sustained success of reform.

When the management objective has been set and stated in that way, managers and their teams can make the five decisions that will shape the communication plan. They'll pass these decisions along to their communication specialists, who then will formulate a detailed communication plan with timelines and budgets (Cabañero-Verzosa 2002, 2005; Cabañero-Verzosa and Elaheebocus 2008). Here are the five decisions, briefly stated:

1. Whose support is critical to the reform's success?
2. What behaviors must be adopted to achieve the reform objectives, and what changes in knowledge and attitudes will facilitate the adoption of those behaviors?
3. What messages will persuade people to support reform?
4. What channels of communication will reach people and be credible to them?
5. How will communication be monitored and evaluated?

The tool shown in figure 1.2 is handy for managers and their teams to use when discussing and arriving at those five decisions. (A template version of the tool that can be copied and used immediately is given at the end of the chapter.) In the following sections, we address the decisions in greater detail.

Decision 1: Whose Support Is Critical?

By identifying groups of people whose support is crucial to a reform's success, managers are able to focus communication resources on those groups. To decide which groups of people are the most valuable supporters at each stage of a reform initiative, it is necessary to segment prospective audiences, distinguish opponents from supporters, and assess their levels of interest and power. Over time, it will be important to revisit this decision, identifying supporters at various stages of the reform.

Segment Audiences. Segmenting audiences is a vital initial task. Strategic communication is less concerned with disseminating massive quantities of information than with analyzing audience perceptions, motivations, attitudes, and behaviors. Therefore, one of the key contributions that strategic communication makes to a reform program is the analytical process used in assessing why people do what they do. That knowledge is quite valuable to reform agents— even more valuable than what reformers envision as desired practices—because

Figure 1.2. Communication Management Decision Tool

Management Objectives:

[Here, describe the goal of the project or policy reform. For example, "increase numbers of girls who complete secondary school."]

Audience	Behaviors	Messages		Channels	Evaluation
		Takeaway Message	Supporting Data		

Source: Cabañero-Verzosa 2002.

it provides a basis for segmenting a reform's audiences into distinct focal groups.

One way to segment audiences is to identify primary, secondary, and tertiary audiences. A primary audience is a group of people whose behavior the program must influence. In a pension reform project, for example, self-employed workers who are not contributing regularly to the pension fund may have to be motivated to do so. In a water supply project, residents in urban areas may be asked to reduce waste by fixing water leaks immediately. In a privatization project, policy makers may be encouraged to vote for increased private sector participation in the country's telecommunications industry. A reform's primary audience is not always obvious. In a Bangladesh project intended to increase secondary school completion among girls, communication research helped the team understand the cultural values and decision-making dynamics within the family. When the research revealed that the primary audience consisted of fathers, rather than mothers, communication materials were designed to persuade fathers to send their daughters to school.

A reform's secondary audience comprises those influencers who exert pressure on the primary audience either to accept or to reject the new behavior. In the case of Bangladeshi fathers who were struggling with the decision to go against traditional practices, their decision was influenced mainly by other older men in the community.

The tertiary audience consists of those who wield influence over communities because of their status as leaders, those who have access to resources that can be directed toward reform, or those who are able to persuade large groups of people because of their credibility and charisma.

Communication activities must be customized to meet the information needs of these various audience segments. Primary audiences need information about how they will benefit from reform to help them make individual decisions on whether they will take action or adopt the desired behaviors. Secondary audiences must be motivated to support adoption of new practices by members of the primary audience. Tertiary audiences have to be prompted to take action at a community, regional, or national level. For example, policy makers (a tertiary audience) must promulgate new policies that provide an enabling environment so primary audiences who are ready to accept reforms and engage in new practices receive the services and access to resources that will make it possible for them to undertake new behaviors successfully.

Identify Opponents and Supporters. To complement the audience segmentation approach, project teams may assess political economy issues relevant to their various audiences. Some groups will be interested in a reform issue, some will be disinterested fence-sitters, and others may be strongly opposed to a reform program for ideological and other value-laden reasons. A clear lesson learned from political communication is that communication efforts need to be focused on the "swing constituencies" because these groups are more likely to be persuaded about the benefits of reform than are those who are strongly opposed for ideological reasons.

A targeting strategy (figure 1.3) helps managers determine the nature and level of attention they need to direct to these various groups. At both ends of the audience continuum are groups who need minimal communication effort: At one end, hardcore allies are firmly committed to change and may need minimal information about progress and remaining challenges. At the other end are immovable opponents who may need information about the proposed change, but whose opposition may be based on deeply held beliefs and values that are contrary to the change initiative. People in the middle of the continuum require more communication effort: Those who are uncommitted but involved in the issue may need persuasive messages to encourage their active participation as champions of change. Those who are uncommitted and uninvolved may require more time and communication resources than usually are available to reformers. Allies need communication to reinforce their beliefs and encourage their

Figure 1.3. Audience Targeting Strategies

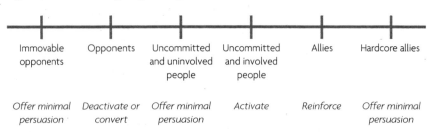

Immovable opponents	Opponents	Uncommitted and uninvolved people	Uncommitted and involved people	Allies	Hardcore allies
Offer minimal persuasion	*Deactivate or convert*	*Offer minimal persuasion*	*Activate*	*Reinforce*	*Offer minimal persuasion*

Source: Gary Orren, Kennedy School of Government, Harvard University, Cambridge, MA, 2002.

Figure 1.4. Audience Interest/Power Analysis Matrix

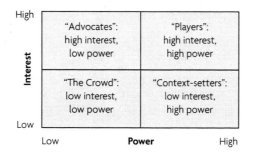

Sources: Authors' illustration, with reference to Lindenberg and Crosby (1981) and Moore (1995).

active involvement in advocacy and the implementation of reform measures. Opponents may be converted to support the cause; or, if it is unlikely that their opposition can be addressed to their satisfaction, communication efforts will aim to neutralize the negative impact of their opposition.

Assess Audiences' Interest and Power. Deciding which audience groups have both interest in and power over a reform issue helps reform agents allocate communication resources more effectively. The 2-by-2 matrix presented in figure 1.4 separates audiences in four quadrants and identifies them according to their levels of interest and power: those groups with high power and high interest ("players"), with low power but high interest ("advocates"), with low interest but high power ("context-setters"), and with low interest and low power ("the crowd").

Analyzing audiences according to their levels of interest in the reform issue and their levels of power to promote or derail reform enhances a manager's ability to set priorities for allocating communication resources to those groups with the most power and interest in the issue. It also helps a manager customize communication activities to the specific needs of the four types of audiences. A reform manager must understand why the reform may be considered salient by some groups but not by others; and he or she must assess which groups have the power to influence reform, either positively or negatively.

Groups with high power and high interest in the issue should be accorded serious communication attention. These groups are engaged directly in the development and implementation of reforms. These groups consist of critical decision makers with the power to provide or withhold resources or to veto a change initiative. In development programs, this may include the minister of finance who decides on the allocation of funds to projects and policy reforms. It also may include the line ministry responsible for the sector—such as health, education, agriculture, and infrastructure—who may oppose the proposed program or policy option. People with low interest and high power may have little interest but may be able to unleash their potential power over an issue if the reform attracts their interest and attention at some point in the reform process. For example, members of the media may not be interested in a reform initially; but if conflict and controversy arise around the reform, they may use their power to reach national and international audiences with messages that portray the reform program as a failure. Thus, reform managers need to monitor how context-setters react to the reform at its various stages. Advocates have no formal authority to approve reform measures, nor do they have resources to allocate to change initiatives. These groups may have deep knowledge of the issues and can capture the attention of policy makers, the media, and the general public; but they have no formal authority or financial resources to fund reforms. Civil society organizations and private sector business and professional associations are examples. Although advocates have high interest in an issue, they likely will not participate directly in the decision making and their power over the reform is limited to advocacy and persuasion. For example, civil society members who are invited to observe public bidding for government contracts may be intensely interested in transparency and governance, but are not likely to have a direct influence on the outcomes of public bidding processes carried out by government agencies. They can press for increased transparency, but they have no institutional authority to select a winning bidder. Finally, there are those groups who neither are interested in nor have influence over a specific reform. Although they are not organized around the issue being addressed and the reform currently is not important to them, they must not be ignored out of hand because they can be activated by advocates or context-setters. When mobilized, "the crowd" can drive public opinion, strengthen the voice of advocates, join hands with the context-setters—and focus strong public will on a reform issue. The communication strategy designed for a reform agenda must address all four sections of the interest/power matrix.

Identify Crucial Stakeholders at Different Stages of Reform. Reforms take shape over a period of time and are championed by different stakeholders at various stages. A communication strategy should be appropriate for the stage of reform and must address people's evolving understanding and perceptions about the reform as it unfolds.

Naim (1993) describes two main stages of economic reform: (1) achievement of macroeconomic stability and (2) development of institutional capacity in the public sector to implement the reform. The shift from one stage to the next is not always defined clearly and there will be some overlap. For example, efforts to stabilize macroeconomic factors through such measures as fiscal adjustment and exchange rate management will have to continue at the same time that attention is focused on institutional development. Naim warns that "institution building in the public sector is less amenable to the kinds of blunt and very visible solutions that tamed macroeconomic stability." Consider Latin America. The major goal there in the 1980s was macroeconomic stability, but it now is seen only as a precondition. Creating and rehabilitating institutions needed to sustain growth is "the more difficult part of the equation" (Naim 1993).

The role of communication changes at various stages of economic reform. The first stage of economic liberalization often involves high-level government officials who issue decrees or executive orders to revise the rules that govern macroeconomic behavior. The urgency of the situation may provide little opportunity for broad-based participation by the general public, the business sector, and the government bureaucracy. Political will to undertake reforms is nurtured among key leaders in government and powerful elites in the private sector, and expedient action is taken to get legislation passed. Thus, communication efforts are highly targeted to these powerful individuals and elites, such as in lobbying activities to secure passage of legislation. At the second stage of economic reform, however, institutions that will implement the reform and their respective constituencies are involved. And there is the difficult task of managing people's expectations about the costs and benefits of reform. At this second stage, a communication strategy will address many more audiences holding different perceptions and predispositions toward taking the needed actions that will contribute to the reform's success. The Philippine procurement reform case study, presented in chapters 6 and 7 of this volume, describes the communication strategy for two phases of governance reform: the first phase focused on getting an omnibus procurement reform law passed through three changes in political leadership in the country, and the second phase concerned with implementing reform nationwide.

Decision 2: What Changes in Knowledge, Attitudes, and Behaviors Will Lead to the Success of the Reform?

Successful reforms involve many people—from leaders in government and the private sector, to the institutional heads who must implement reforms, to various political constituencies, civil society organizations, communities, households, and individuals. A communication strategy must identify clearly which behaviors by which groups of people will contribute directly to the success of a reform. During the first stage of reform (at the macro level, as it is called in table 1.1), when the objective is to provide the policy framework for national programs to reduce poverty, the behavior change goals may involve policy makers enacting new laws. In the second stage of reform (the micro level, as it is termed in table 1.1), when policy implementation takes place, the communication goal will be to get more people to adopt different but complementary behaviors that contribute to the reform's success. For example, in implementing reform after the procurement law was passed, the Philippine government team had to embark on two sets of communication activities. It had to build understanding of and support for reform among government staff in the various national ministries directly involved in enforcing the new law; and it had to address the information needs of the local government units, civil society organizations, media, and general public who interact with government and the business sector.

In large-scale reforms, managers naively may assume that informing people of the new law will ensure ready compliance. In that vein, many communication programs are aimed at generating awareness about a problem, advocating reform, and threatening punishment for those people who contravene the reform. General awareness-raising campaigns have a role in the reform process, but project teams often mistakenly assume that those information dissemination activities will lead to changes in knowledge, attitudes, and behaviors that contribute to the success of reforms. There are many examples of development programs in which communication activities are aimed only at increasing people's awareness of issues that reforms seek to address, with little thought given to how communication can be used to involve people who begin to grow interested in the issue and are motivated to seek solutions and take action at either the individual or the community level. But people change gradually, and communication must be synchronized accordingly. Recognizing that people become aware of an issue, gain knowledge about it, develop an interest in it, revise their attitudes, and change behavior in stages offers managers a more realistic yardstick for assessing how swiftly reform may capture people's imaginations, prod leaders to champion it, and mobilize citizens for action.

Drawing on evidence of how people change addictive behaviors like smoking and on the stages of change, Prochaska, di Clemente, and Norcross (1992) developed the transtheoretical model to describe the process people go through in adopting and maintaining new behaviors. The authors identify five stages of behavior change: precontemplation, contemplation, preparation, action, and maintenance. Applying that concept to work in development reform and knowing the various stages of change for critical stakeholders will help program teams hone their messages for greatest efficacy and success.

An effective communication strategy synchronizes communication activities to support people at various stages of change. Its activities can increase people's understanding of issues and persuade them that the issues are personally relevant. If people are motivated to try new behaviors, communication activities can give them information on the location of and access to relevant public services. When people already are engaged in trying new behaviors, the activities can encourage them to maintain those behaviors, acquainting them with others who have adopted new practices successfully and thus assuring them that social norms are evolving to support their new behaviors.

As can be seen in table 1.1, the communication strategy must address people's unique communication needs as they progress through the various stages of change—from being unaware (precontemplation stage); to gaining awareness (contemplation); to understanding the issue and the proposed solution

Table 1.1. Characteristics of Behavior Change Stages and Appropriate Strategies for Communicating and Eliciting Participation

	Behavior Change Stage				
	Unaware	Aware	Understand	Adopt	Sustain
Characteristics of a person at this stage	• Is ignorant, uninformed • Resists change • Engages in unsafe/risky practices	• Is informed, knowledgeable • Is aware of benefits of behavior change • Is aware of need to learn new skills	• Appreciates benefits of behavior change • Is motivated to adopt new behavior	• Decides to take action • Tries new behavior	• Consistently practices new behavior
Communication strategy for this stage *Macro level:* policy/sectoral reform	Awareness raising and sensitization: • increase public and stakeholder awareness through public information campaign	Information sharing and education: • build understanding • establish two-way communication to address concerns and perceived problems • conduct public communication activities • implement outreach program • open a national dialogue program • engage with media	Motivation: • build consensus to maintain dialogue • build communication capacity through training sessions • conduct public relations activities • hold advocacy campaign	Trial and adoption: • build ownership of the reform • build social partnerships • create constituencies for reform • encourage public involvement	Maintenance and monitoring: • build commitment to the reform • support constituencies for reform • analyze content and reach of media coverage of reform
Micro level: project intervention	• Raise awareness • Conduct sensitization and advocacy campaigns • Hold media training for reformers to help them work more effectively with media	Launch multimedia campaigns to increase knowledge, build new skills, and promote benefits of reform	• Continue multimedia campaigns • Set up peer-group counseling • Conduct community mobilization	• Encourage continued use of tangible product or services or promote adoption of new policies and procedures needed to implement reform measures by emphasizing benefits	• Reiterate benefits of new behavior • Reinforce ability to sustain behavior • Sustain social support

(continued on next page)

Table 1.1. Characteristics of Behavior Change Stages and Appropriate Strategies for Communicating and Eliciting Participation (continued)

	Behavior Change Stage				
	Unaware	Aware	Understand	Adopt	Sustain
Strategy for eliciting participation in this stage	• Orient media professionals on reform issue Information sharing: • dissemination of information materials • public meetings • presentations, seminars	Consultation: • meetings • field visits and interviews	Cooperation: • participatory assessments/evaluations • beneficiary assessments	• Enlist early adopters to model new behavior • Offer social support Collaboration: • joint committees with stakeholder representatives • stakeholders given principal responsibility for implementation	Empowerment: • capacity building of stakeholder organizations • management by stakeholders

Source: Garcia and Cabañero-Verzosa 2004.

(preparation); to adopting new beliefs, attitudes, and behaviors (action); and, finally, to sustaining practice over time (maintenance). Communication activities also may vary, depending on whether they are targeted at the macro level (policy/sectoral reform) or at the micro level (project-specific interventions).

Decision 3: What Messages Will Persuade Audiences to Support the Reform?

Communicating the benefits as well as the costs of reform in ways that resonate with various stakeholders and audiences is an important element of a reform's communication strategy. Message development generally is deemed the communication specialist's domain, but reform managers play a crucial role as well. The "message" here refers to a takeaway message, not to the organization's message about reforms. Rather than communicating an organization's message, the concept of a "takeaway message" is at the heart of an audience-oriented mindset. The basic proposition is that communication efforts have a better chance of helping people gain new knowledge, adopt positive attitudes, and try new behaviors if they start from the position of the audience perspective rather than that of the communicator.

Rather than focusing on what they want to say to various stakeholders, reform managers should begin the process of message development by asking these questions: What reform benefits are meaningful for stakeholders? How can we discuss these benefits so that stakeholders will find the messages credible? What supporting data can the reform agencies provide to help stakeholders see these benefits and be convinced that they will receive them if they change their beliefs, attitudes, and behaviors?

Reformers often focus their messages on the benefits they themselves perceive as resulting from reforms, mostly from a technocratic perspective. The messages then offered to stakeholders are based on logical, cogent arguments. Such organization-centered messages may not resonate with audiences and stakeholders for a number of reasons. For example, stakeholders may not recognize the problem that reforms are seeking to address, so benefits ushering from proposed reforms seem to bear no relevance for them. Even if stakeholders agree that the problem exists, they may not see the technocratic solution as feasible and so mistrust reformers who promise results that they themselves have not seen or experienced. Messages that appeal to both the hearts and the minds of stakeholders are more effective.

Decision 4: What Channels of Communication Will Reach Audiences and Be Credible to Them?

Communication channels are the various ways that messages are disseminated to different audiences. In deciding which mix of communication channels will be effective in a given reform, there are three aspects that reformers must bear in mind: reach, frequency, and credibility.

Reach is the extent of a particular medium's coverage. In other words, how many people in the target audience or stakeholder group are exposed to the message? For example, in a country with almost 90 percent radio penetration, this channel of communication will have a broader reach than, say, printed newspapers that are available only in capital cities and are read mainly by the literate elites. Another aspect of reach is the ability of a communication channel to access audiences when they are most receptive to the message and are close to making a decision relevant to the message being communicated. Frequency is the number of times that people in the target audience or stakeholder group receive messages about the reform. There is an advertising principle that communicators use: the more people who are reached by a given message and the higher the frequency of their exposure, the greater the probability that those people will respond. Hornik (2002) notes that in the field of public health, where communication has been used extensively to promote behavior change, weak emphasis on the primary goal of ensuring high levels of exposure over extended periods of time is a "crucial failing" (p. 13).

Credibility is the perception by audiences and stakeholders that a given vehicle (that is, radio, television, print) provides balanced reporting of events and that messages carried there are not influenced unduly by government or private sector groups who own and operate those vehicles or by other advocacy groups who promote a specific perspective to the exclusion of other views. In interpersonal communication situations, the credibility and trustworthiness of the individual doing the communicating defines the credibility of the communication channel itself.

In many developing countries, an effective mix of communication channels may not be based largely on electronic or mass-mediated vehicles. Traditional communication systems, rooted in a given culture and often having more resonance and credibility, may need to be tapped as well.

Decision 5: How Should Changes in Knowledge, Attitudes, and Behaviors Be Tracked and Evaluated?

In developing a communication strategy, it is useful to start with the end in mind. The final goal of strategic communication is to foster change in the knowledge, attitudes, and behaviors of specific audiences and stakeholders. Hornik (2002), discussing public health communication campaigns, identifies three complementary models of behavior change that also are valuable to managers of various types of reform. First, he notes that individuals change behavior as a result of their exposure to messages aimed at influencing their individual behavior. Second, behavior change occurs among social groups, so communication programs aimed at changing social norms then influence social groups to adopt new behavior. Third, an institutional diffusion model focuses on changing elite opinion, which influences institutional behavior such as enactment of new policy. In both the social norm change and institutional change models, individuals change behavior because it is the expected response to changed social norms or policy.

The model of behavior change used in designing and implementing communication activities influences the type of evaluation that needs to be done to measure changes in knowledge, attitudes, and behaviors among audiences and stakeholders as a result of communication activities. Two types of evaluation approaches may be of practical value to reform managers. The first type is descriptive: it documents changes in knowledge, attitudes, and behaviors over time. The second type not only documents change, but also attempts to measure the extent to which change can be attributed to the intervention (CommGAP 2007). The second approach is more complex, more expensive—and more desirable when feasible. Studies that attribute changes in knowledge, attitudes, and behaviors to communication interventions may use experimental or quasi-experimental designs. Or they may use only postintervention data, but combine them with statistical analysis to establish an association between the communication intervention and the outcome.

The limitation in evaluating communication interventions is the difficulty in isolating the effects of communication activities from secular trends. Communication often is embedded in a larger social change intervention, and it is difficult to isolate effects of communication from effects of other components of the larger intervention (CommGAP 2007).

Hornik (2002) advises that despite the difficulties in isolating communication effects, it is valuable to evaluate communication interventions if the evaluation tells policy makers how worthy of support a particular reform and its attendant communication activities are, if it guides the design of future reforms, and if it respects "the way that communication programs in real life are likely to affect behavior" (Hornik 2002, p. 405).

Using Strategic Communication in Real-Life Reform Programs

In this volume, we want to examine the design and efficacy of strategic communication in various reform efforts. We use the case studies of actual reform programs presented in subsequent chapters to do that. Because the communication strategies embedded in reforms rarely are described in project documentation and therefore are not available to us here, we are providing an ex post description of how communication management decisions likely were made when the communication strategy was designed. We have gathered several examples of reform initiatives and will demonstrate that the communication management decision tool (figure 1.2) can be used to articulate key decisions that shaped the communication strategy. In subsequent chapters, we present the following examples: projects, economic and sector work, and a Country Partnership Agreement (formerly referred to within the World Bank as a Country Assistance Strategy). The sample of reform initiatives includes

- investment climate reform in Bosnia and Herzegovina (chapter 2)
- Moldova's poverty reduction strategy (chapter 3)
- Peru's Accountability in Social Reform (RECURSO) project (chapter 4)
- the 2006–08 Country Assistance Strategy for the Philippines (chapter 5)
- public procurement reform in the Philippines (chapters 6 and 7)
- the West African Gas Pipeline Project (chapter 8).

These case examples demonstrate how project teams, reformers, development practitioners, and policy makers effectively can use the Five Communication Management Decision tool to formulate a communication strategy. With that handy and practical tool, reformers may be systematic and disciplined in their communication efforts, using their scarce communication resources to achieve development results. The core principles of strategic communication are embedded in these management decisions. Specific communication activities that are in accordance with these management decisions will be "strategic," whereas communication activities that are not in accordance will be "off strategy" and will not merit allocation of communication resources.

Notes

1. The terms *audience, stakeholder,* and *client* are used interchangeably to refer to the parties whom reformers wish to influence. Messages are targeted to audiences. Stakeholders are consulted and engaged in dialogue and debate about policy change or program design. Clients are provided tangible services, such as education or health care.
2. A communication-based assessment enables managers to obtain necessary information on stakeholder attitudes, perceptions, and practices as well as the sociocultural and political environments that influence the development program. A detailed approach is described in Mitchell and Chaman-Ruiz (2007).

References

Cabañero-Verzosa, Cecilia. 2002. "Determinants of Behavioral Intention in Developing Country Organizations." Doctoral diss., Department of Communication, University of Maryland, College Park, MD.

———. 2005. *Counting on Communication: The Uganda Nutrition and Early Childhood Development Project.* World Bank Working Paper 59. Washington, DC: World Bank.

Cabañero-Verzosa, Cecilia, and Nawsheen Elaheebocus. 2008. "Strategic Communication in Early Childhood Development Programs: The Case of Uganda." In *Africa's Future, Africa's Challenge: Early Childhood Care and Development in Sub-Saharan Africa,* ed. Marito Garcia, Alan Pence, and Judith L. Evans, 331–52. Washington, DC: World Bank.

CommGAP (Communication for Governance and Accountability Program). 2007. *Evaluation Framework for Governance Programs: Measuring the Contribution of Communication.* CommGAP Discussion Papers. Washington, DC: World Bank.

Garcia, Helen R., and Cecilia Cabañero-Verzosa. 2004. "From Outreach to Outcomes: Integrating Communication in Social Assessments." Unpublished manuscript, World Bank, Washington, DC.

Hornik, Robert C. 2002. *Public Health Communication: Evidence for Behavior Change.* Mahwah, NJ: Lawrence Erlbaum Associates.

Lindenberg, Marc, and Benjamin Crosby. 1981. *Managing Development: The Political Dimension.* Piscataway, NJ: Transaction Publishers.

Mitchell, Paul, and Karla Chaman-Ruiz. 2007. *Communication-Based Assessment for Bank Operations.* World Bank Working Paper 119. Washington, DC: World Bank.

Moore, Mark H. 1995. *Creating Public Value: Strategic Management in Government.* Cambridge, MA: Harvard University Press.

Naim, Moises. 1993. *Paper Tigers and Minotaurs: The Politics of Venezuela's Economic Reforms.* Washington, DC: Carnegie Endowment for International Peace.

Prochaska, J. O., C. C. di Clemente, and C. Norcross. 1992. "In Search of How People Change: Applications to the Addictive Behaviors." *American Psychologist* 47 (9): 1102–14.

Decision Tool:

Management Objectives:

-
-

Audience	Behaviors	Messages		Channels	Evaluation
		Takeaway Message	Supporting Data		

2

The Bulldozer Initiative:
Investment Climate Reform in
Bosnia and Herzegovina

In 1995, the signing of the Dayton Peace Accords created a new central state
government and two independent entities—the Federation of Bosnia and
Herzegovina and Republika Srpska. The peace agreement also brought together
three distinct ethnic groups—the Muslim Bosniaks, the Orthodox Serbs, and
the Roman Catholic Croats.

The years of war preceding the peace agreement had caused serious economic decline and extensive loss of physical capital. The international community
provided substantial support to mount large-scale postreconstruction work.
External financial and technical assistance focused on rebuilding the economy
and restoring physical and social infrastructure, including power, public works,
transportation, housing, agriculture, health, and education.

Much was achieved after several years of working toward peace, political stability, and economic recovery. The macroeconomic situation stabilized and sectoral reforms in public finance and the social sectors were implemented. The
country experienced a threefold increase in GDP, a tenfold increase in mer-
chandise exports, and a steady increase in foreign direct investment.

Despite those achievements, however, progress in key areas continued to lag
behind that of neighboring countries. Broad structural reforms aimed at building a market economy stalled because of divided political leadership and fragmented constituent groups. Although the privatization of the banking sector
was successful, the divestiture of large enterprises faltered. A complex bureaucracy and cumbersome business practices remained as major disincentives for
much-needed private sector investments. And as foreign aid continued to dwin-

dle, the country's greatest challenge of boosting private sector activity remained. In 2004, four out of 10 people in the labor force are out of work and seeking jobs. Without the promise of employment opportunities, poverty rates currently estimated at 20 percent of the population may increase (Herzberg 2004, p. 4).

Broader, more vigorous stakeholder involvement was needed to accelerate the pace of reform. Largely skeptical of the government's commitment to change, the general population viewed the international community as the principal change agent responsible for carrying out reforms. In particular, the High Representative was regarded as the key authority figure responsible for implementing the civilian provisions of the peace agreement and vested with the power to issue laws and regulations.

Project Profile

In November 2002, the Office of the High Representative launched the Bulldozer Initiative, a landmark undertaking aimed at building a grassroots constituency to speed up the pace of economic reform. The specific goals of the initiative were to (1) "bulldoze" through bureaucratic red tape and simplify businesses practices and (2) build a strong working partnership between the government and the private sector. To implement the initiative, the High Representative began the creation of a Bulldozer Committee comprising business representatives and four international assistance agencies—namely, the European Commission, the International Monetary Fund, the U.S. Agency for International Development, and the World Bank.

Instead of introducing large-scale reforms that often are politically contentious, the initiative pursued a strategy of going for small and incremental yet critical changes to promote a more favorable business climate. The focus was on supporting overall reform efforts by introducing specific legislative amendments to remove obstacles in business practices. Reform implementation involved three key phases.

Phase I

Phase I of the reform focused on engaging representatives of the private sector and soliciting their reform proposals to address bureaucratic red tape. The immediate challenge was the business community's distrust of government. Because of its corrupt practices and strong vested interests, the government lacked credibility and public confidence in its commitment to undertake meaningful reform. To build a strong constituency of supporters within the private sector community and to lend much-needed credibility and legitimacy to the effort, the Office of the High Representative had to assume the role of active sponsor and to play a key and visible role.

The Coordination Unit within the Office of the High Representative solicited reform proposals from the business community. Submissions poured in from various groups of entrepreneurs and business associations. Through painstaking advocacy work, broad support was generated from private sector groups. The Bulldozer Committee, which was responsible for reviewing the proposals and introducing reform measures, grew to include members who were staunch advocates of the initiative.[1]

Proposals were presented and publicly discussed in plenary sessions where some 40–50 representatives from the business community participated and voted on the proposals. The Bulldozer Committee then reviewed and endorsed the proposals. The committee, the Bosnia and Herzegovina Council of Ministers, and the governments of the Federation of Bosnia and Herzegovina and Republika Srpska held intensive discussions and negotiations on specific reform proposals. This productive dialogue led to parliamentary approval of the first package of 50 reforms under Phase I.[2]

Phase II

Phase II, launched in June 2003, maintained the momentum of progress from Phase I. The goal of this phase was to identify another set of 50 reforms. Committed to supporting the interests of the business community and local advocacy groups, the second phase focused on building a strong partnership with elected officials, including the trade unions. A decentralized approach to identifying new reforms (depicted in figure 2.1) highlighted the important role of regional governments. Six regional committees representing local businesses in

Figure 2.1. Phase II: The Bulldozer Reform Process

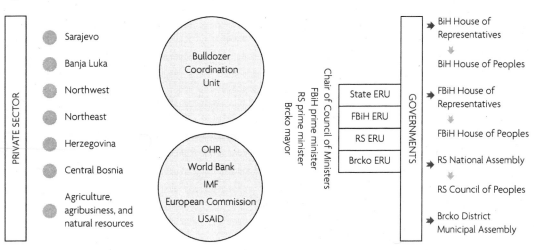

Source: Herzberg 2004.
Note: BiH = Bosnia and Herzegovina; ERU = Emergency Reform Unit; FBiH = Federation of Bosnia and Herzegovina; IMF = International Monetary Fund; OHR = Office of the High Representative; RS = Republika Srpska; USAID = U.S. Agency for International Development.

each geographic area and a specialized national-level Committee on Agriculture, Agribusiness, and Natural Resources were created. These committees were responsible for generating proposals for Phase II and implementing the reforms of Phase I. This collaboration strengthened the three-way partnership among the private sector, the regulatory agencies, and the unions and public advocacy groups.

The private sector representatives are organized into regional committees that partner with an Emergency Reform Unit for each government jurisdiction. A Coordination Unit monitors and regulates the process, while serving as the point of contact with the international organizations (Herzberg and Wright 2005).

In response to the increasing public support for the reform, the three prime ministers, the six heads or speakers of the three parliaments, the mayor of Brcko, and the seven local Bulldozer Initiative representatives signed the Protocol for Prosperity agreement. Subsequently, Emergency Reform Units were created at the state level, and an interministerial working group shared the task of soliciting and reviewing proposals. The group worked closely with the local and regional private sector committees.

Phase II successfully concluded with a second package of 50 reforms for parliamentary approval and the eventual phasing out of the international community's veto power in the reform selection process.[3] The institutional foundations set in place provided the framework for building local capacity and further stimulated public dialogue to form broader constituencies of support at the grassroots level. With the government and the private sector working as partners, the reform implementation not only accelerated in pace but also widened in scope. The final list of 50 reforms encompassed areas other than business (such as guaranteeing the rights of disabled people and establishing national holidays) to benefit various sectors of civil society.

Phase III

Phase III marked the start of a locally driven initiative. In December 2004, the Office of the High Representative officially transferred management authority for the Bulldozer Initiative to the Bosnia and Herzegovina Employers' Confederations. Although the international community has relinquished its leadership role, it continues to provide support through technical assistance. The goal of this phase was to sustain a working public-private partnership, one kept strong and effective through active and productive dialogue. Ultimately, the grassroots constituencies of support built through the early phases of the initiative may evolve from strong advocates of small, incremental changes into key interlocutors in the larger arena of broad-based structural reforms.

Table 2.1 presents the three phases of the initiative, their overall themes, and the reform actors involved in each phase.

Table 2.1. Initiative Phases, Themes, and Actors

Actors	Phase I: 50 Economic Reforms in 150 Days	Phase II: Unlocking Local Wealth	Phase III: Minding Our Own Business
Executing agencies	• Bulldozer Committee	• Bulldozer Committee, including regional committees • Emergency Reform Units at the state level	• Bosnia and Herzegovina Employers' Confederations
Stakeholders	• Private sector • Regulatory bodies	• Private sector • Regulatory bodies • Trade unions	• Private sector • Regulatory bodies • Trade unions
Direct beneficiary groups	• Private entrepreneurs	• Private entrepreneurs • Local business associations • Civil society	• Private entrepreneurs • Local business associations • Civil society

Source: Authors' compilation.
Note: The thematic descriptions of the three phases of reform were taken from the Bulldozer Initiative Web site.

Obstacles and Opportunities

The Bulldozer Initiative faced a difficult reform environment. Political leadership, undermined by a strong ethnic divide and vested interests, posed risks to the reform agenda. People were skeptical of the government's commitment to reforms and doubted its ability to carry out a meaningful process of change. Lack of clear understanding of the goals and benefits of reform resulted in public opposition and indifference toward key policy efforts. The international community was perceived to have sole responsibility for initiating reforms—in particular, the High Representative, who had the authority to enact and repeal laws.

The public's strong, negative attitude had to be addressed because broad support for and ownership of reforms were key elements underlying the Bulldozer Initiative's successful implementation. There was strong skepticism and a lack of faith in the bureaucracy. Local businesses had to be convinced that significant changes could be achieved and that benefits could be gained through the active involvement of local entrepreneurs. One of the first challenges was to raise public awareness and secure buy-in from the local entrepreneurs who would play a central role as key advocates of change. To meet this challenge, strategic communication was employed.

Role of Strategic Communication

The initiative's primary goal was to "bulldoze" bureaucratic red tape as a means to improve the business climate and create an investor-friendly private sector environment. Making the case for the reform had to start with clear understanding of the existing problems and the benefits reform could bring to individual businesses and the economy as a whole. Creating that understanding presented an important opportunity to mount a strategic communication effort aimed at raising public awareness, educating key stakeholders, building consensus through public dialogue, and engaging businesses as the key drivers of change.

Raising Public Awareness

To build grassroots support and improve public perception, the initiative launched an extensive public awareness campaign. An advocacy brochure titled "Bulldozer Initiative: 50 Economic Reforms in 150 Days," written in the Bosnian, Croat, and Serb languages, was distributed widely (84,000 copies). It presented a detailed description of the 50 reforms selected in Phase I. These reforms had been analyzed carefully and selected after several public consultations held across the country. The brochure explained each reform proposal in a clear and concise manner, identifying the problems and describing the proposed solutions (see box 2.1 for an example).

A key complement to the brochure was a comic strip called "The Adventures of Max," which featured the life of a frustrated entrepreneur whose problems were solved by joining the Bulldozer effort (box 2.2). Max, the comic strip char-

---

Box 2.1. Reform No. 24: Easing Export of Drugs and Medicine from Bosnia and Herzegovina

The Situation: The pharmaceutical industry is a very successful export industry in the country. It is very important to the BiH economy, and it provides many jobs. Pharmaceutical companies rely on their ability to export their products and samples quickly, efficiently, and on time to foreign partners and buyers. However, in December 2002, the Council of Ministers changed the regulations governing the import and export of medical products. Now an additional export license is required from the State Ministry of Foreign Trade and Economic Relations, in addition to the licenses obtained from the Entity Ministries of Health for these and other goods.

Why is it a problem: This decision has added a step in obtaining the license, another unnecessary procedure which takes valuable time from entrepreneurs. The process takes 10–15 days more for purely procedural reasons. Nothing changes; the same license is issued on a different letterhead. These unnecessary but extensive delays reduce BiH's competitiveness in the export market.

The solution: Entity Health Ministries should continue giving the licenses. These ministries should be obliged to send an ex-officio copy to the Ministry of Foreign Trade and Economic Relations for their information/statistics. This would remove the burden from the entrepreneur and result in less time lost.

What do the current requirements mean for your company?

"Since January this year we have not been able to meet the deadlines promised to foreign partners and we are losing business. The new administrative barrier added in December 2002 has made exporting even MORE difficult for us than before!"– Edin Arslanagic, CEO, BOSNALIJEK

Amendments to be enacted in BiH: CoM Decision on amendments and changes to the Decision on classification of goods for export and import regime (Official Gazette BiH 40/02, Item 3).

Source: "Bulldozer Initiative: 50 Economic Reforms in 150 Days" brochure, p. 29.
Note: BiH = Bosnia and Herzegovina; CEO = chief executive officer; CoM = Council of Ministers.

Box 2.2. MAXimizing Reform through Comics

Through *The Adventures of Max*, a comic strip series for adults, the Bulldozer Initiative turned the entrepreneur into the hero. The main character, Max, not only dramatized how regulations hurt the average person trying to do business in the private sector, but also educated people about the reforms and the reform process. Even though Bosnia and Herzegovina had no history of adult comics, "Max" was widely read.

The strip tells the tale of a young man—a former rock star—who wants to start an insulation business but discovers how hard it is to get through all the red tape required for setting up a legal company. The first "Max" story was published as part of an advocacy brochure explaining the 50 reforms that had been proposed, and was distributed to more than 80,000 people. The second "Max" story, which centered on an argument between Max and a government official over the value of the reform effort, was distributed in 200,000 copies of the brochure and was sent to newspapers. The Bulldozer Initiative, with strong public support, pushed through 50 reforms in just over 150 days.

Source: Knowledge Services for Private Sector Development, World Bank.

acter, added a human dimension to the reform process as his life story created a personal illustration of the adverse impact of a bad business environment on a typical local entrepreneur.

Educating Stakeholders

A handbook on privatization—*What It Is, How It Works, Why Should I Care*—also was widely circulated (200,000 copies) to inform and educate local businesses and the public. Simple, easy-to-understand, and visually interesting, the handbook focused on the benefits of privatization and the key elements of success. And to the unconvinced business owner or skeptic, the message was simple: "More investment, more production, more jobs, more exports, more tax revenue, and more regional development. The list of benefits is long. That is why it is crucial to move the privatization process forward with renewed energy."

As an information and education tool, the handbook used real-life examples of successful local businesses and explanations of how privatization made a significant difference for them to counter the lack of public confidence in achieving tangible reform results. Testimonials from key stakeholders (investors, union leaders, and local government authorities) made it clear that these three reform actors had to work together to ensure a successful privatization effort.

Box 2.3. Message to the Local Entrepreneur

What Do I Do Next?

An essential part of any movement for economic change is the effort to create new legislation. To do this, you must know how to communicate your issues. The Bulldozer Roadblock Submission Form will help you do that.

Help your representatives in their decision-making process.

You have an important role to play in the decision-making of your representatives. It is impossible for them to have access to all of the information relevant to what is happening in the economy or to understand fully the implications of legislation for the everyday life of BiH citizens. You can provide important information to your elected representatives so that their deliberations and decisions are a result of a thorough review of the relevant issues. You provide a critical perspective since you are the closest individual to the market and the economic reality.

You also have the right to express your support for or opposition to legislation.

Communicating your ideas through the Bulldozer Committee in your region can have an enormous impact. Detach the form at the end of this brochure and send it to the collection point closest to you.

Source: "Bulldozer Initiative: 50 Economic Reforms in 150 Days."
Note: BiH = Bosnia and Herzegovina.

The public awareness campaign stressed the accountability of local entrepreneurs and their central role in helping improve the business climate. It stressed the importance of active participation by local businesses as a means to ensure the reform's sustainability.

A special section in the "50 Economic Reforms in 150 Days" brochure addressed two key questions relevant to the local businessperson: "What does this have to do with me?" and "What do I do next?" It urged readers to communicate their ideas and suggestions, and it walked them through the process of using the Bulldozer Roadblock Submission Form. The campaign made clear why local entrepreneurs needed to lobby actively for the adoption of the proposed changes. (Box 2.3 presents the brochure's answer to the second question.)

Building Consensus through Dialogue

Two-way communication among policy makers, political leaders, and key stakeholders ensured broad public consensus and helped create constituencies supportive of reform. Although informing and educating the business community and key stakeholders was necessary, it was not sufficient to ensure the success of the initiative. Local entrepreneurs also were engaged and given a venue for expressing their views in an open, public dialogue.

Public participation in reviewing and selecting proposed reform changes was made possible by the involvement of more than 20 organizations from various parts of the country. Acting as public sector representatives in the Bulldozer Committee's Plenary Session, various organizations had the opportunity to express their views on proposals requiring legislative amendments. After much debate and deliberation, the voting session on the final list of proposed reforms was aired on prime-time news programs. This balloting broadcast demonstrated the openness and transparency of the entire process.

A series of road shows also served as venues for public gatherings and to rally people to action. Presentations reinforcing the messages communicated in the public information brochures were made at public meetings held in eight different cities. More than 500 businesspeople were present at these events.

Mobilizing the Media

The vigorous public awareness campaign was one of the main pillars of the communication plan. The initiative's media strategy tapped journalists and members of the media as a key channel in effectively communicating the progress of reform. Here are several aspects of the strategy:

- An open-door policy with journalists allowed journalists easy, transparent, and regular access to ongoing developments in the Bulldozer Initiative. They received unfiltered news, both positive and negative. Press interviews, briefings, and informal breakfasts kept journalists up to date on the progress made in the reform.
- Press conferences were conducted as part of all significant initiative events. Journalists and members of the media joined the Bulldozer Committee and covered landmark events consisting of the public information meeting, the plenary session meeting, and the voting on reforms. They also were present during the committee's preliminary work completion, the government handover of the reforms, and the entrepreneurs' explanation of the reforms to the three parliaments.
- Symbolic treatment of major initiative achievements was an important media strategy to document historic and memorable events (see box 2.4). The press and media representatives covered commemorative occasions in symbolic settings.

Through the media's involvement, the Bulldozer Committee's work under the initiative gained high visibility and helped maintain national interest in key reform issues. There is continuing public engagement, and the members of the local business community are kept abreast of outstanding legislative improvements.

Lessons Learned and Challenges Remaining

Although the initiative's well-designed communication plan helped influence many local entrepreneurs' changes in attitude and behavior, negative sentiment continued in some sectors of society. Critics and opposition groups led anti-Bulldozer campaigns to discredit the initiative's leaders and goals (table 2.2). Many opponents questioned the reform's real impact on the economy and doubted the initiative's grassroots focus. Taking a forthright approach, the Bulldozer Committee dealt head on with the issues. Complete and accurate facts were provided to clarify certain misconceptions and engage the public in open and constructive dialogue. This response helped deactivate some of the fierce opposition and successfully converted some strong opponents into sympathetic allies.[4]

Given this backdrop, table 2.3 shows how the communication management decision tool could have been developed to support the reform process, partic-

---

Box 2.4. The Bulldozer Initiative's Symbolic Events

The press conference organized in front of a real bulldozer became a turning point in the political life of Bosnia and Herzegovina. For the first time, the chair of the Council of Ministers made a public and formal commitment with businesspeople: together, they would enact 50 reforms in 150 days, and reforms would be judged on their merits rather than on internal politics (as is often the case in the country).

The photo of the prime minister wearing a red construction helmet appeared on the front pages of all the nation's newspapers on the day after the press conference. The media began to cover entrepreneurs in a positive way. Instead of portraying them as "crooks trying to benefit from the system," the media described them as "frustrated stakeholders eager to take over the future of their country." One major newspaper began to run a daily column featuring local entrepreneurs and the changes in legislation they would like to see. This new approach was a true awakening for Bosnia and Herzegovina businesses, and the resulting change in public opinion had lasting impact.

Another symbolic event took place at the National Theater. The initiative brought together all the parliaments of state, entity, and district jurisdictions to discuss with the Bulldozer Committee the merits of the reforms. This was the first time these parliaments had gathered since their creation by the Dayton Peace Accords in 1995.

The Protocols for Prosperity were signed at the Botanical Gardens. The Protocols was the first document since the peace treaty to bear the signatures of all heads of the executive and parliamentary bodies. To mark the event, each of the 17 signatories planted a rose tree in an area that was named the "Prosperity Garden."

Source: Herzberg 2004.

Table 2.2. Interests and Actions of Opposition Stakeholders

Stakeholder Group	Issues and Basic Interests
Chambers of commerce	• Resented the reduced scope of their functions that resulted from the initiative; opposed potential loss of income from mandatory fees that resulted from the reform proposal.
Political leaders	• Feared the loss of political power resulting from reform proposals that promote deregulation and feared disruption in the country's state of affairs.
Government	• The Ministry of Foreign Trade and Economic Relations, in particular, resented the reform's proposed policy on the delivery of export certificates because it implied the ministry's lack of competence.
Some members of the local and international community	• Doubted that the bottom-up process of reform was genuine; questioned the initiative's scope of work as appropriate and the timeline of 150 days as achievable, and predicted its failure in implementation; dismissed the possibility of any far-reaching and significant impact because of the reform initiative's narrow scope.

Source: Herzberg 2004.

Table 2.3. Decision Tool: Bulldozer Initiative

Management Objectives:

- To raise public awareness and build grassroots support for legislative amendments needed to improve the business environment
- To foster productive dialogue and partnership between government and the private sector

Audience	Behaviors	Messages		Channels	Evaluation
		Takeaway Message	Supporting Data		
Council of Ministers, government, relevant ministries	• Conduct active and open dialogue with private sector representatives	• "Government needs to hear the views of the private business community. Public-private dialogue is a critical step in the reform process."	• Technical studies • Private sector assessments	• Meetings and consultations • Workshops and seminars	Enhanced dialogue: • number of government officials who conducted dialogues with private sector group • quality and number of proposals submitted by the private sector • number of opposition groups who support reform and advocate adoption of legislative amendment
Private entrepreneurs and business community	• Support reform efforts in bulldozing bureaucratic red tape and recommend proposals to improve the business climate	• "Bureaucratic red tape should be eliminated to save businesspeople time and money, which they can use to grow their businesses. Private entrepreneurs should help identify administrative bottlenecks, propose legislative solutions, and lobby for their adoption."	• Enterprise surveys • Consultations	• Press conferences • Informal breakfast meetings	

(continued on next page)

Table 2.3. Decision Tool: Bulldozer Initiative (*continued*)

| Audience | Behaviors | Messages | | Channels | Evaluation |
		Takeaway Message	Supporting Data		
Opposition groups	• Actively engage in public debate to understand both the adverse consequences of outdated laws and administrative barriers and the benefits of reform • Support reform to improve the country's overall economic development	• "I will support reform initiatives to improve the business climate and advocate adoption of legislative amendments. These initiatives will provide substantial economic benefits and will not necessarily mean a loss of power among political leaders or a lack of competence among regulatory and technical agencies of government."	• Focus group • Public opinion survey	• Brochures, handbook, and information materials • Road shows and public events • Print media • Meetings and consultations	

Source: Authors' compilation.
Note: LGU = local government unit; NGO = nongovernmental organization.

ularly in addressing reform resistance and in building stakeholder-specific support for the Bulldozer Initiative.

The initiative benefited from innovative approaches to creating public awareness and mobilizing grassroots reform committees to build a broad constituency of support. The initiative's communication strategy provides the following key lessons of experience:

- Clarity of objectives and mapping of strategic approaches provide a clear road map to achieve the expected results.
- Open consultations and regular communication in the early stages of reform increase public trust and encourage public involvement.
- Creative and selective use of audience-targeted communication tools and techniques is a powerful means of informing, educating, motivating, and influencing attitude and behavior change.
- Unique and strong positioning establishes a reform's "brand" through the effective framing of messages.
- Use of credible reform messengers strengthens the public trust and enhances the perceived legitimacy of a reform, which is especially important in a communication environment weighed down by detractors and opponents.
- Early and continuous involvement of the media helps stimulate public interest in reform issues and sustain active stakeholder engagement over the long term.
- The two-way flow of communication achieves the positive public engagement necessary to build consensus, stakeholder ownership, and accountability.

An early assessment of the Bulldozer Initiative's implementation results revealed that Phase I reforms helped improve the country's business climate. Accomplishments included creating more jobs, increasing tax revenues, generating capital for investment, and boosting exports. Reduced administrative burden and a shrinking gray economy restored investor confidence and boosted the reform's credibility among local entrepreneurs.[5] Although the overall impact of the Bulldozer reforms has yet to be realized fully, the initiative has been successful in changing the attitudes and mindset of the business community and of the public at large.

Notes

1. The committee comprised 30 local groups, including regional business associations, municipal associations of entrepreneurs, the Association of Honey and Bee Production, the Central Bank, the Employers' Confederations of both the Federation of Bosnia and Herzegovina and Republika Srpska, the Foreign Investment Promotion Agency, the Micro-Credit Network, and the Women's Business Network (Herzberg 2004).
2. Phase I's package of approved reform proposals included changes to address issues concerning enterprise operations, the environment and forestry, tourism, labor, trade, registration, chambers of commerce, finance, and transportation (Herzberg 2004).

3. The second round of 50 reforms addressed issues concerning administrative requirements, enterprise, finance, forestry/environment/agriculture, investment, labor, trade and utilities, and construction.

4. One of the most outspoken opponents was a Serb Nationalist Party official who later supported the initiative after meeting with the regional Bulldozer Committee coordinators.

5. Investors were convinced about the Bulldozer process of eliminating bureaucratic bottlenecks. For example, Horizonte, an Austrian investment fund, reopened its operations after two years of business inactivity. The Austrian Bank HVB, a proponent of Phase II reforms, doubled its investments in Bosnia and Herzegovina through its acquisition of National Profit Banka.

References

Herzberg, Benjamin. 2004. "Investment Climate Reform—Going the Last Mile: The Bulldozer Initiative in Bosnia and Herzegovina." Policy Research Working Paper 3390, World Bank, Washington, DC.

Herzberg, Benjamin, and Andrew Wright. 2005. "Competitiveness Partnerships: Building and Maintaining Public-Private Dialogue to Improve the Investment Climate—A Resource Drawn from the Review of 40 Countries' Experiences." Policy Research Working Paper 3683, World Bank, Washington, DC.

Moldova's Economic Growth and Poverty Reduction Strategy

3

Since its independence in 1991, Moldova's transition to a market economy had been slow and difficult on many fronts. An agriculture-based economy with a small population of about 4.3 million people, Moldova underwent an economic collapse triggered by substantial fiscal deficits and a buildup of external debt. The country's economy suffered an external shock from the 1998 financial crisis in the Russian Federation and the secession of the Transnistria region in the early 1990s, which resulted in the loss of Moldova's economic base in the energy and industrial sectors. The steep economic decline of 60 percent led to a subsequent rise in poverty levels. In 1998–99, about 73 percent of the population was estimated to be living below the poverty line.

Political uncertainty and unforeseen institutional changes also contributed to the country's poor transition performance. In mid-2000, Parliament approved a major amendment to the Constitution, changing Moldova from a presidential to a parliamentary republic. Parliament's failure to elect a new president led to its dissolution, and general elections were held in February 2001. Subsequently, a new president was elected, a new government was formed, and the Communist Party of Moldova gained a stronghold after winning the majority of votes.

Despite the positive experience of a healthy electoral process, the political environment remained uncertain. Successive changes in governments led to significant interruptions in the transition process. Progress faltered and the results were disappointing. The international donor community's enthusiasm to offer support waned. The government had to demonstrate its commitment to pursuing the required structural reforms to complete its transition to a market economy.

After a decade of poor performance, the government's intensified efforts led to a stabilization of the economy and to sustained implementation of structural reforms. In 2000, the country was on the threshold of an economic upturn. Successfully pulling out of its deep, postindependence slump, the economy has grown at an average rate of 6–7 percent since 2001, with the industrial sector registering the fastest growth. This growth was accompanied by a significant rise in the level of investment, from 11 percent in 2001 to 16 percent in 2003. Workers' remittances, valued at $286 million, fueled increases in consumer spending and have been the largest contributor to the country's economic recovery. However, despite macroeconomic reforms and economic restructuring, the anticipated benefits from a growing economy have not generated the impact necessary to reduce poverty, especially among the most vulnerable rural households.

Profile of the Poverty Reduction Strategy Process

The volatile political circumstances of the 1990s delayed the preparation of the first Poverty Reduction Strategy Paper (PRSP) for Moldova. The Interim PRSP completed in 2000 was shelved for one year because of the parliamentary crisis. In August 2001, the government resumed the PRSP preparation process, and a revised Interim PRSP was approved in 2002. Committed to developing a comprehensive framework for sustainable growth and poverty reduction, the government adopted the Economic Growth and Poverty Reduction Strategy Paper (EGPRSP) in 2004 (World Bank 2004), as the first full PRSP for Moldova. Accomplished through a highly participatory process, the development of the strategy was supported by an institutional structure that facilitated communication within government and with key development partners and various civil society representatives (figure 3.1).

Support for the development of the strategy was provided at the highest level of government. The National Council for Sustainable Development and Poverty Reduction, chaired by the president, served as the main coordinating body for the strategic planning of Moldova's long-term and medium-term socioeconomic development. To ensure the development, promotion, and implementation of the strategy and other related strategic plans, the Interministerial Committee for Sustainable Development and Poverty Reduction was created as the executive body.

The Participation Council was established to ensure the broad-based participation of civil society and to foster regular and productive dialogue with other key stakeholder groups. The council comprised representatives from the public sector (state and local institutions), the private sector, relevant nongovernmental organizations (NGOs), and international donor organizations. A Grant Implementation Unit, established as the Participation Council's exec-

Figure 3.1. Institutional Framework for EGPRS Development

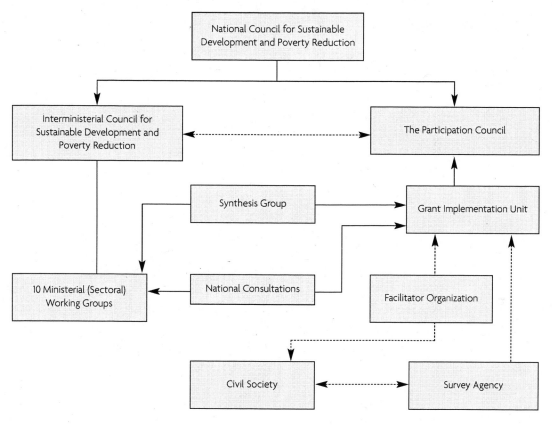

Source: Mozammel and Odugbemi 2005.
Note: EGPRS = economic growth and poverty reduction strategy.

utive body, primarily was responsible for managing the trust funds provided by international organizations to support the development of the strategy. In 2003, the Participation Council approved an action plan to guide the implementation of participatory activities organized in three successive phases: (1) a public information campaign and needs assessment, (2) public participation in formulating the economic growth and poverty reduction strategy, and (3) identification of mechanisms for stakeholder participation during the implementation and monitoring phases. To coordinate the range of activities at the national and local levels effectively, the Network of Non-Governmental Organizations was selected as the facilitating organization. It served as the focal point and facilitated the process of organizing all participation and communication activities.

The Ministry of Economy, as the overall coordinator of the strategy, led the substantive and technical work, with the support of two core teams: the Synthesis Group prepared the overall strategic framework and the Sectoral Working Groups tackled specific sectoral issues, strategies, and proposed action plans.

Obstacles and Opportunities

The stop-and-go cycle of strategy formulation marked a period of delays and of overcoming roadblocks as the country undertook its first full poverty reduction strategy process. The state of political flux in the 1990s led to frequent changes in political leadership that disrupted and delayed the country's smooth market transformation. This flux resulted in high staff turnover and the steady erosion of a trainable cadre of officials capable of providing intellectual and technical support to a government engaged in a dynamic process of change.

Weak institutional capacity was a serious roadblock in the preparation process. The technical and administrative staffs involved had limited skills to undertake the diagnostic and technical work needed to prepare the strategy, and they were not familiar with the processes required to develop such a comprehensive strategy. For a country having limited experience with broad consultations, the highly participatory process added to the challenge of expediting its successful completion. Some government authorities were reluctant to engage stakeholders in a transparent and open dialogue. The Soviet legacy of centralized planning and top-down decision making became a difficult barrier that had to be addressed, especially among traditional bureaucrats and conservative political leaders. To help break this barrier, extensive consultations were held to address their concerns and broaden their understanding of the benefits of participation. The discussions with the public authorities clarified the objectives and scope of participation and provided a good opportunity to identify suitable participation mechanisms.

The Participation Council—with its broad representation from various sectors of government, the donor community, and civil society—was an effective venue to facilitate these two-way exchanges. The dialogues opened up opportunities to underscore the advantages of civil society engagement in developing the strategy: (1) gaining a better understanding of the poverty in Moldova, (2) promoting positive interaction between the government and society, (3) fostering a meaningful dialogue in defining priorities for public action, and (4) ensuring better allocation and use of resources. It also helped the authorities fully appreciate the principles that would guide the conduct of participation activities, which focused on providing transparency in soliciting the views of state institutions and civil society, documenting the participation activities, and disseminating through the mass media the results of public forums and the input of stakeholders at various consultations. Subsequently, the gradual shift in the behavior of authorities toward civil society involvement became evident in the expanding scope of public participation—from a narrow, less inclusive approach in the early stages of drafting to an extensive, broad-based strategy of public consultations and communication leading up to the final completion stage. Table 3.1 presents a timeline of the key communication interventions made since October 2002, and table 3.2 provides illustrative detail concerning the audience-targeted communication activities undertaken.

Role of Strategic Communication

Communication was considered an integral part of the strategy formulation process. The goals of the communication campaign were defined clearly: (1) in-

Table 3.1. History of Moldova's Communication Interventions

Date	Item	Who	Quantity	Distribution
October 2002	Roundtables with civil society and government officials	DFID	2, about 120 participants in all, representing all sectors of NGO work	Organized in Chisinau, the capital city, with invitees from the regions
November 2002	Poverty forum	Government of Moldova and WB	Circa 150 participants	Organized in Chisinau
March 2003	Second Poverty forum	Government of Moldova and WB	Circa 100 participants	Organized in Chisinau
August 2003	Video clip advertising the EGPRS	Produced by OWH TV Studio	1	Broadcast so far on Euro TV channel (capital coverage)
2003	Documentaries	Produced by OWH TV Studio	2	Broadcast on National TV channel (national coverage)
September 2003	"Tell Poverty No" booklet	Elaborated by GIU	160,00 copies, in Romanian, Russian, and English	Distributed at all participation events and through other channels
September 2003	"Tell Poverty No" poster (in the state language only)	Elaborated by the OWH through the DFID grant, endorsed and promoted by the government and GIU	2,000 copies	Distributed at all participation events and through other channels.
October 2003	EGPRS Web site	Created and run by GIU	1	Can be visited by those with Internet access—mainly in the capital city and larger settlements
October 2003	EGPRS newsletter	Created by the Association of Independent Press on behalf of the GIU	4 editions, 77,200 copies each, in Romanian and Russian	Nationwide, as a free supplement to the local and national newspapers, members of the Association of Independent Press
2004	Briefing with the media	GIU	n.a.	n.a.
17 December 2003–10 January 2004	National seminars	Government of Moldova, GIU	10	Chisinau, with key stakeholders to present the draft EGPRS
27 January–10 February 2004	Local roundtables	The Women's Forum, under the contract with the Ministry of Economy, GIU	9	Across the country, to start the consultation
Since mid-2003 until now (ongoing)	Journalists are invited to the meetings of the Participation Council, press releases by GIU and sent to media outlets	GIU	n.a.	Chisinau

Source: Mozammel and Odugbemi 2005.

Note: DFID = U.K. Department for International Development; EGPRS = economic growth and poverty reduction strategy; GIU = Grant Implementation Unit; n.a. = not available; NGO = nongovernmental organization; WB = World Bank.

Table 3.2. Communication Activity Plan

Strategic Approach	Target Group	Tools	Terms
Administrative mobilization	• Parliamentarians • Parliamentarians • Sector working groups • Mayors • Political parties • NGOs	• To elaborate leaflet for parliamentarians • To elaborate a database, including fax numbers, emails of parliamentarians in order to inform them periodically about the EGPRSP elaboration process • To ensure the public is informed on how the feedback provided is taken on board • To send by mail the information about EGPRSP and to ask their involvement through accumulating opinions of citizens; roundtable with participation of mayors' associations • Roundtable with the participation of political parties' representatives; to include parties in our email group and to send periodically information about EGPRSP • To send draft sector strategies and the government strategy and to discuss with them; to invite NGOs' representatives to participate in seminars and roundtables organized within the participation process; permanent communication by email, telephone	1–15 March 2004 15–29 February 2004 27 January–30 March 2004 25 February 2004 22–28 March 2004 20 February 2004 1 February–30 March 2004 27 January–13 May 2004
Social mobilization	• Youth, parents, teachers • General public	• To organize the essay contest for pupils from schools, high schools, and residential institutions • To promote the Web site forum in order to accumulate public opinions • To publish the sector strategies résumé in the national mass media • To publish in national and local media articles and analysis regarding the EGPRSP • To edit the EGPRSP bulletin	1 February–2 April 2004 Permanent 13 February–30 March 2004 Permanent 12 February–5 March 2004
Advertising/ publicity	• General public	• To place the video spot on national TV channel • To organize the show "Buna Seara" dedicated to PRSP process • To organize 2 special TV shows with the participation of the minister and other invitees • To organize 6 radio shows (OWH TV Studio) • To realize 1 TV show dedicated to PRSP and to place it on local channels • To organize interactive shows on national radio • To print and place stickers in city transport • To promote the site in national media • To place billboards	February–April 2004 March 2004 February, March 2004 February–May 2004 March 2004 February–May 2004 March 2004 February–March 2004 March 2004
Interpersonal communication	• Mass media • National and local coordinators of the facilitator organization	• To invite mass media to national and local activities • To organize a contest for journalists • To organize press briefings and press conferences • To organize nonformal meetings with journalists • To inform about messages at each stage • To send the media list with all local journalists	Permanent February–April 2004 3 February 2004, 30 March Permanent Permanent January 2004
Point-of-service promotion	• Public • Academia, the public	• To distribute the information through information points throughout the country • To print and place the strategy in public libraries	Permanent February 2004

Source: Mozammel and Odugbemi 2005.

Note: EGPRSP = Economic Growth and Poverty Reduction Strategy Paper; NGO = nongovernmental organization; PRSP = Poverty Reduction Strategy Paper.

form the public about the importance of public participation; (2) encourage public debates on issues, strategies, and policy options; and (3) foster civil society participation to ensure wide ownership of the process. Much of the focus was on creating awareness through information dissemination activities, building public consensus through consultations, and maintaining public involvement through appropriate communication techniques.

In the early years of preparation, public participation was limited and fragmented. To give added impetus, the donor community played a strong partnership role in supporting communication events that helped broaden access to information. In 2002, the World Bank provided assistance for conducting poverty forums, videoconferences, and workshops, and the U.K. Department for International Development financed a project by the OWH TV Studio (a Moldovan NGO) to conduct a communication campaign.

When the draft strategy was completed in December 2003, participation and communication activities were launched in three stages: (1) informing the public about the preparation process, focusing on stakeholder feedback on the issues and proposed solutions, through 10 national seminars and nine local-level roundtable discussions; (2) gathering stakeholder input on the draft strategy through 36 participation activities consisting of seminars and roundtable discussions held at national and local levels; and (3) providing feedback to stakeholders on the results of their contributions and soliciting comments on their involvement in the EGPRSP implementation through another round of 36 national and local discussion forums.

Targeting Audiences and Behaviors

Public authorities at all levels were identified as the most important target audience. Changing the behavior of this segment of the population was a key objective of the communication effort. Public authorities needed to understand the benefits of participation before they could believe in and support it. Interpersonal communication and targeted communication events at national and local levels, focusing on specific audience segments and appropriate communication approaches, helped authorities gain that understanding.

At the national level, ministerial discussions were held to establish a clear and common understanding of the strategic goals, the policy measures, and the sector programs for achieving sustainable growth and reducing poverty. National seminars and roundtable meetings provided venues for discussions with key stakeholder representatives from the business and academic communities, think tanks, donor groups, and international organizations. They openly provided feedback on issues pertaining to the EGPRSP diagnosis, objectives, priorities, and monitoring indicators.

In April 2004, the government organized a national forum to present the EGPRSP. The participants provided additional comments, and civil society representatives welcomed the inclusion of relevant recommendations in the draft document and called for continuing public debates. As a follow-up to the forum, workshops were held at the national level to finalize the strategy based on feedback received during the public consultations.

Information and promotional materials with motivational messages designed to target all 900 mayoralties and local public authorities were distributed at the local level. In addition, seminars and roundtable consultations with local public sector employees and civil society representatives from the business community, local NGOs, trade unions, churches, media, and community organizations representing socially vulnerable groups were organized around thematic issues to focus stakeholder feedback on key sectoral issues and priority strategies.

Moldovan youth were considered to be both an audience for and a channel of communication. Representing 25 percent of the population, the youth are among the country's most vulnerable stakeholder groups; their participation in public affairs, however, is almost negligible. The EGPRSP communication strategy also focused on this population group, and the message to the youth emphasized taking personal responsibility for promoting the process of participation at all levels of society. A national essay competition, called "A Solution for My Country," was launched to gain insight on young people's perspectives and encourage them to articulate their views on the challenges facing the country and potential solutions to be considered. The competition was successful in broadening engagement beyond the 560 people who submitted essays because it involved their parents, teachers, and fellow students.

Building Country Ownership and Accountability

Engaging civil society not only raised people's awareness of PRSPs and increased the value of public participation in building ownership and consensus; it also established a systematic information exchange between and among stakeholder groups, a process that is crucial in ensuring transparency and good communication flow. The institutional mechanisms to support strategy development opened avenues along which key stakeholders were able to engage actively and contribute as informed participants to the public debate and policy dialogue. Within the institutional framework, the Network of Non-Governmental Organizations was responsible for collecting stakeholder feedback generated at the events and for transmitting it to the Synthesis Group, which reviewed the comments and incorporated the input as appropriate.

A separate section in Annex 8 of the final PRSP for Moldova offered detailed documentation of the scope and content of public reactions gathered over a 3-month period (January–March 2004). Excerpts from that section (box 3.1) illustrate the breadth of stakeholder input received and the relevant comments that were incorporated in the final draft.

Box 3.1. Stakeholder Recommendations Incorporated in the EGPRSP

Public sector reform:

- Rename the chapter to "Legal Sector Reform" (replacing judicial, which is a limiting approach)
- Create a National Institute of Justice (magistracy) for an ongoing professional training of legal staff (p. 263)
- Optimize the study program and plans for the legal education system.

Infrastructure development:

- Install meters for an efficient use of natural gas, water and heating resources it was (p. 364,b)
- Develop a tariffs system with the simultaneous introduction of the protection mechanism of people with low incomes for an efficient collection of payments for water and energy resources supply (p. 367, v, p. 387, ii)
- Incorporate energy conservation as an efficient means of cost reduction and promotion of public information on conservation methods (p. 364, b, ii)

Education strategy:

- Include in the vocational education system children with special educational requirements for their utmost integration into the society (p. 507, vi)
- Prioritize allocation of resources for salary increases of employees in the education sector (p. 506, iii, 509, v)
- Create the appropriate legal framework to support the community's role (local public administration, parents, economic agents, etc.) in school financing, the (p. 506, i)
- Improve assistance to children with special educational requirements and establish a tracking system to monitor their progress (p. 508)

Social protection, social assistance and labor market

- Orient social aid to the most vulnerable social layers and develop poverty criteria and official threshold of poverty (p. 552, p. 554 ii, p. 560, p. 105, p. 501)
- Create community centers for the provision of medical-social services to people with special requirements (p. 557, p. 564, 556)
- Increase the access of disabled people to the labor market (p. 580)

Implementing, monitoring and evaluating EGPRSP:

- Strengthen Participatory Council as a mechanism to ensure the participation
- Develop a mechanism of interaction between the national and local levels in the implementation, monitoring and evaluation of the EGPRSP

Source: Moldova EGPRSP, Annex 8.
Note: EGPRSP = Economic Growth and Poverty Reduction Strategy Paper.

Creating Public Consensus and Managing Expectations

In promoting country ownership through a participatory process, it also was essential to use the participation and communication processes to manage public expectations. One of the pitfalls of broad-based participation is the risk of unrealistic expectations among stakeholders with different interests, needs, and aspirations. A two-way process of communication is needed to establish, at the outset, a clear and common understanding of the scope, objectives, roles, and responsibilities of key actors and the expected outcomes of public participation.

In the Moldova EGPRSP, the public consultations created stakeholder knowledge and understanding of the issues, strategies, risks, and rewards of key policy choices. This approach helped provide a realistic view what was feasible and achievable, given the country's existing constraints and challenges. Maintaining credibility and legitimacy is critical in building public trust in the process.

Building Momentum through Social Mobilization and Media Activities

Engaging social networks within civil society helped broaden public outreach and enhance the communication environment, especially among local-level stakeholders. Social networks, local NGOs, and the media were effective channels of communication. Particularly effective as a conduit was the Network of Social Area NGOs, which was selected to facilitate the participation events. The network's good relationships with grassroots organizations encouraged participation, even among NGOs that were skeptical of the process.

In addition, a roster of journalists and media representatives and a database of more than 800 NGOs and initiative groups were compiled and used as the distribution list for disseminating to respective stakeholder groups informative notes and press communiqués, including invitations for organized events. In the process, the various groups also received stakeholder feedback that they, in turn, communicated to the responsible authorities.

Appropriate media vehicles were used to support the public information and communication campaign, including radio and television broadcasts. Printed materials—brochures, leaflets, and posters—distributed during organized public consultations and social events reinforced the information transmitted via electronic media. An official bulletin, published in the state language (Romanian) and in Russian, was distributed widely. It contained updated information on the process of participation and on progress in preparing the EGPRSP.

Recognizing the power of Internet communication technology, the government also launched an EGPRSP development Web site. Available in Moldova's state language, as well as in Russian and English, the Web site was designed to expand the sphere of public participation, ensure full transparency, and make the EGPRSP development process accessible to online communities both inside and beyond Moldova. Although many people questioned this move because of limited Internet access within Moldova, the Web site nonetheless signaled the government's commitment to broad participation and information sharing through the use of nontraditional channels of communication.

Lessons Learned and Challenges Remaining

Despite Moldova's weak institutional capacity and unambiguous reluctance to adopt a participatory process, the government turned its limitations into opportunities and successfully pursued the unfamiliar and uncertain path of participation and active civic engagement. Numerous difficulties were encountered along the way, especially in the early stages of preparing the EGPRSP. Insufficient knowledge about participation in policy making led to problems triggered by a lack of credibility and trust in the process, resulting in (1) the limited involvement of and support from the national media; (2) the lack of initiative among civil society groups, especially those who remained suspicious of the government's motivations; and (3) the skepticism of some NGO members who doubted the credibility of the public events. Although it was a slow and gradual process, the shift in the government's attitude toward broad civil society participation—a shift from guarded reluctance to a cautious acceptance of an inclusive process of strategy and policy formulation—eventually occurred and moved the EGPRSP development process to its successful completion.

Strategic communication was a key driver of meaningful participation in the EGPRSP. The Participation Council approved the Participation Action Plan and the Communication Action Plan as mutually reinforcing and strategic components essential in developing a country-owned strategy for sustainable growth and poverty reduction. Sharing information and building public awareness were the first critical steps in ensuring effective communication. With free and open access to information, stakeholders were able to engage effectively in the policy process as informed citizens. Participatory approaches fostered public debates, and the feedback mechanisms provided a systematic process of gathering stakeholder input and informing stakeholders of responsive actions taken. The strategic approach to communication fostered a two-way exchange of information that helped create public consensus, establish country ownership, manage public expectations, and build trust and confidence in the poverty reduction strategy process.

Key lessons from Moldova's early experience with communication highlight the importance of (1) targeting the right audience with the right messages, (2) mobilizing social networks and local civil society groups as active channels of communication, (3) creating communication capacity through the permanent mechanisms that promote two-way communication flows between policy makers and civil society, (4) developing an active and vigilant media to serve as watchdogs in the arena of public debate, and (5) building a strong and cohesive network of civil society organizations as credible partners in the policy process. These lessons offer invaluable opportunities for further strengthening strategic communication efforts in implementing and monitoring the EGPRSP.

The strategy document outlined specific sectoral strategies that explicitly identify communication and access to information as key elements in the implementation phase. For example, public sector reform requires increased public communication and participation to address the problem of limited openness and transparency. Permanent consultation groups comprising national and local authorities and civil society organizations will be established within the public sector to ensure continued public consultations and communication. Key sectors of civil society are expected to have increased access to public administration activities through the Internet and mass media. Local public administration bodies will be encouraged to use broadcast media (press, television, and radio) to inform the public about policies and programs.

Communication also will play a key role in the country's fight against corruption. The draft National Strategy for Corruption Prevention and Fighting Economic Crimes contains three pivotal provisions that call for (1) free access to information, (2) the promotion of coalitions among groups with similar interests in preventing corruption, and (3) creation of communication channels to inform public authorities of corruption cases and to offer protection to people who provide information. Other sector strategies call for greater efforts at information, communication, and participation—namely, private sector development, external trade promotion, financial sector development, agri-food sector and rural development, health care, education, youth development, and social insurance.

Moldova's experience in formulating its first full PRSP prompted the development of a consultation culture through extensive public participation and the strategic use of effective communication approaches. Although the process paved the way for some meaningful behavior change among key actors involved, many challenges remain on the road to implementation. The final measure of success will be translating the long-term strategy into long-term development results, especially those benefiting the poor and most vulnerable groups in Moldovan society. Central to achieving this ultimate goal is the country's ability to mainstream participation through permanent institutional mechanisms and to enhance the culture of consultation through an enabling environment supported by strategic communication.

Table 3.3 illustrates how the decision tool could have been applied in the preparation of a communication strategy for the Moldova EGPRSP.

References

Mozammel, Masud, and Sina Odugbemi. 2005. *With the Support of Multitudes: Using Strategic Communication to Fight Poverty through PRSPs*. London: Department for International Development.

World Bank. 2004. "Moldova: Poverty Reduction Strategy Paper and Joint IDA-IMF Staff Advisory Note of the PRSP." Report 29648. World Bank, Washington, DC.

Table 3.3. Decision Tool: Moldova's EGPRSP

Management Objectives:

- To build ownership by critical stakeholders of the country's poverty reduction strategy through public information and public participation during the various stages of development
- To promote public discussion and deliberation among key stakeholders to thresh out important issues and concerns and formulate a poverty reduction strategy that is supported by broad public consensus

Audience	Behaviors	Messages		Channels	Evaluation
		Takeaway Message	Supporting Data		
• National government: president, Parliament, ministries of economy and finance • Coordinating agencies: National Council for Sustainable Development and Poverty Reduction, Participation Council • Local public authorities • Public sector employees	• Conduct broad-based consultations in the formulation of the EGPRSP • Adopt policies that promote active participation of all sectors of civil society • Design and implement mechanisms to facilitate public engagement in EGPRSP formulation • Participate actively in public consultations • Help broaden public understanding of the EGPRSP and its objectives	• "Engagement of civil society in EGPRSP formulation is critical in fostering public trust and support. A transparent and inclusive process will help shape a strategy based on the informed participation of the broad sectors of civil society." • "Good communication builds the ownership necessary to ensure accountability and successful implementation of PRS objectives." • "Local authorities should serve as key facilitators in government's efforts to broaden public participation in EGPRSP formulation."	• Technical studies • Public opinion polls	• Meetings and consultations • Workshops, seminars, and conferences • Stakeholder consultations • Roundtable discussions	• Government action on institutional mechanisms for public participation • Technical input from sectoral ministries and specialized agencies

(continued on next page)

Table 3.3. Decision Tool: Moldova's EGPRSP (continued)

Audience	Behaviors	Messages		Channels	Evaluation
		Takeaway Message	Supporting Data		
Civil society: • NGOs • Trade unions • Business community • Academic community and professional organizations • Opinion leaders • Grassroots organizations representing poor communities and socially vulnerable groups	• Actively engage in public consultations and mobilize networks to help disseminate information about the EGPRSP • Contribute to the development of the EGPRSP through substantive discussions, and stimulate informed public debate on important issues • Encourage public participation in EGPRSP consultations among local communities	• "Civil society organizations are key partners in EGPRSP formulation. As facilitators and watchdogs of the participatory processes, civil society should help organize activities and monitor progress to support public information and communication for the EGPRSP." • "Active participation in the consultation process is essential to help identify the special needs of vulnerable groups and to develop appropriate strategies for intervention." • "Media support is necessary to help broaden the reach of public information activities and to promote productive dialogue among stakeholders."	• Technical studies • Public opinion polls	• Stakeholder consultations • Roundtable discussions • Community meetings and consultations • Press conferences • Promotional materials and information brochures • Print media	• Government action on institutional mechanisms for public participation • Technical input from sectoral ministries and specialized agencies • Media monitoring

Media			
• Use mass media channels of communication (print, broadcast, Internet) to disseminate information about the issues and concerns of government officials, civil society groups, and individuals regarding the EGPRSP formulation • Provide balanced reporting of issues • Encourage various sectors of society to discuss and debate issues so as to lead to broad-based support for the rationale and goals of the EGPRSP	• Technical studies • Public opinion polls • Media interviews with government officials, civil society organization leaders, and individuals	• Press materials provided by government and civil society organizations	• Media coverage—reach, frequency, and quality of reporting (assess if reports were balanced, providing both sides of an issue)

Source: Authors' compilation.
Note: EGPRSP = Economic Growth and Poverty Reduction Strategy Paper; NGO = nongovernmental organization; PRS = poverty reduction strategy.

4

Accountability in Social Reform in Peru: The RECURSO Project

Peru experienced political turmoil following unprecedented events in 2000. After two consecutive terms as the country's president, Alberto Fujimori's third-term electoral victory in 2000 ended abruptly because of a widely disputed re-election process and a major corruption scandal. This led to the fall of Fujimori, ending his 10 years of political leadership. A transitional government took over and, in 2000, newly elected President Alejandro Toledo assumed office, taking on a five-year term.

The Fujimori regime left a legacy of strong economic policy, a focused poverty reduction program, and domestic security brought about by the successful termination of the country's most notorious guerrilla movement. In the early 1990s, Peru had a robust economy, with GDP growing by 5.8 percent annually and high investment growth. Despite the country's economic strength, however, other important aspects of Peruvian society were neglected. The transitional government inherited a system plagued by weak public institutions, ineffective regional and local governments, and fragile democratic processes.[1] The country had struggled through the external shock of the 1998 recession, which weakened terms of trade and increased the cost of external financing. In 2001, Peru's estimated debt profile was at 50 percent of GDP, or 3.2 times exports of goods and services. Increasing poverty, unemployment, and crime threatened the country's

For this case, the key source document is Cotlear (2006). He led the core RECURSO team, which included the contributing authors of this book and an implementation group. The World Bank and the U.K. Department for International Development cofinanced the project.

economic stability and social order. By the end of 2001, more than half of the population (55 percent) was poor, with 25 percent living in extreme poverty.

The Toledo administration took on the difficult tasks of reversing the economic downturn, restoring macroeconomic stability, and providing social assistance—especially for the poor. In 2002, the government signed a two-year stand-by agreement with the International Monetary Fund to support an economic restructuring program. To generate broad consensus amid rising public frustration, the administration conducted consultations with various civil society groups to promote an open dialogue on reforms and public policy. At the national and municipal levels, the administration convened roundtable meetings on poverty reduction. A national dialogue culminated in the signing of the National Agreement among major political parties, unions, and civil society organizations. The agreement embodied a 29-point statement of policies focusing on democracy and the rule of law; competitiveness; equity and social justice; and an efficient, transparent, and decentralized state.

Peru's economic recovery gradually took off, spurred by the government's agenda of fiscal discipline, tax reform, and a sound debt management strategy. Back on track, the economy grew from near-zero growth in 2001 to a robust rate of 4.8 percent in 2004. Despite fiscal retrenchment, the government recognized the importance of increasing social expenditures and protecting priority social programs from budgetary cutbacks. Although social expenditure decreased between 1999 and 2002 (from 19 percent to 17.8 percent of the budget), pro-poor spending was reallocated to protect investments in education, health care, and social assistance programs. The increased social spending in the 1990s had produced improved social outcomes: basic literacy rates rose, and increased immunization coverage and public health interventions reduced child mortality rates. Despite such progress, however, the quality of services continues to worsen.

Project Profile

The National Agreement, signed in June 2002, identified equity and social justice as strategic areas requiring policy action in response to growing public concern. The government launched the RECURSO project (Rendición de Cuentas para la Reforma Social; Accountability in Social Reform) to provide an in-depth diagnosis of the social sector's key problems and challenges. In particular, the study was intended to analyze the primary obstacles, inefficiencies, and institutional difficulties plaguing public service delivery in Peru and to evaluate the impact of social participation. It would use international comparisons to examine historical trends in the distribution of public funds and the achievements made in coverage, quality, and equity.[2]

The RECURSO project was a two-year joint undertaking by Peruvian experts, government representatives, and international development specialists. The project team drew on its collective knowledge and skills in doing the analytical work that would reveal key service delivery obstacles threatening Peru's human development and would help identify appropriate strategic policy actions. The team was organized into six thematic groups: education, health care, social assistance, public expenditures in the social sectors, social participation in the delivery of social services, and the incentive framework for teachers and doctors. On the government side, the national agencies involved were the ministries of finance, education, health, and women and social development; and the Office of the Prime Minister.

Key Approaches

The project incorporated innovative approaches that may be reproducible in other social sector projects. First, the project adopted a blended approach to diagnose problems in each sector, combining traditional technical and economic analysis with an investigation of the institutional issues that impinged on the sector. Where available, an analysis of anthropological data helped reveal people's perceptions of client power, their coping behaviors, and their attitudes toward change.

Second, the project pursued a strategic and thematic focus, with accountability issues as the common thread of analysis. The accountability framework described in the 2004 *World Development Report* (World Bank 2003) was used as an analytical and practical tool to help explain the causes of persistent inefficiencies and inequities in the delivery of social services. RECURSO was the first project to apply the accountability framework in analyzing service provision in a single country.[3]

Third, the project was highly participatory through the various stages of development. Consultations with policy makers, service providers, academics, and members of civil society were held in the planning stage. When the initial stage of analysis was completed, the project team presented the preliminary results and held policy discussions with Peruvian colleagues, counterparts, and key stakeholders. Finally, the team discussed the recommendations with government authorities, political organizations, the academic community, and key civil society representatives.

As a fourth approach, the team crafted a carefully designed dissemination strategy that would ensure effective public outreach. The strategy used various communication tools and methods to inform key audiences and the public about the results of the study. The project used broadcast and print media to reach an estimated 6.8 million people. Meetings and interviews with Peru's policy makers and key members of the project team were covered extensively by the media, with coverage comprising about four hours of television air time and 69 press releases. Media outreach was complemented by interpersonal communication, such as public meetings and consultations that included presentations for leading political groups and local communities. Treating indigenous communities as a specific audience segment, the project launched radio programs in four indigenous languages.

Conclusions and Recommendations

The analysis of each sector revealed that poor service quality and lack of accountability are among the most urgent problems affecting Peru's human resources. Although significant strides have been made in coverage since the 1970s, difficult challenges remain. In education, for example, there is a large gap between enrollment and achievement levels.[4] Despite high completion rates at the secondary level, most graduates have inadequate skills and they are at a great disadvantage in the competitive job market. Among primary-level students, only 25 percent of first-graders and 50 percent of second-graders are literate (Cotlear 2006, p. 81).[5] Using reading speed and comprehension as proxies for the quality of instruction, the study found that children in primary school performed far below the minimum standard. For a country similar to Peru in its level of development, the minimum expectation among reading specialists (such as the National Reading Council in the United States) is a reading speed between 30 and 60 words per minute for all children.[6] Peruvian schoolchildren had an average reading speed of only 9 words per minute at the end of first grade and 29 words per minute at the end of second grade (p. 81). Learning inequality[7] also is higher in Peru than in any other Latin American country, with a performance ratio of 2.8—even higher than the 2.1 performance ratio in Brazil, where income inequality exceeds that of Peru (p. 81). The early reading development study also revealed that teachers tend to apply lower standards on students, a problem worsened by the lack of administrative support or the setting of inappropriate official standards.

In health, unequal access, service quality, and outcomes are the most urgent concerns in Peru. Despite overall improvements, significant inequality exists between the rich and the poor populations. Infant mortality is considerably higher in poor households than in wealthy ones. About two-thirds of the poorest households receive no health care, compared with only 13 percent of rich households (Cotlear 2006, p. 8). In the area of social assistance, the RECURSO study found an uneven coverage of social protection and marginal impact on the poor. Although antipoverty programs reach poor people, they have produced disappointing results in the health and nutrition of young children. Despite several food-based programs, child malnutrition remains high overall at 26 percent; and the poorest children are worse-off, with 47 percent of them suffering from malnutrition.

The most important conclusion of the RECURSO study is that Peru's deteriorating quality of services has reached a low-level equilibrium. Deficiencies in the delivery of public education and health care have economic and sociopolitical antecedents, and they have fostered negative changes in institutional and sociocultural attitudes and practices (see box 4.1). The long-term decline in teacher and health worker wages, demoralization of service professionals, and poor work discipline contribute significantly to negative social outcomes. Similarly, systemic problems of corruption, poor government enforcement, ambi-

guity of rules, and weak user demand for services promote the harmful consequences of low-level equilibrium. The RECURSO study further noted that a
cultural change is necessary to revamp the social service delivery system. In ad-

---

Box 4.1. Attitudes and Practices Resulting in Low-Level Equilibrium

On the low level of commitment:

"Doctors don't want to hear that they have duties as well as rights. They don't respect their
schedule, they punch their timecards and then leave, they skip duty whenever they feel like it,
and they don't even work their full 6-hour shift. They come for short spells, they prefer to teach
at the university. Out of 100 nurses, 80 manage to get sick certificates and skip work."

– Director, large hospital in Lima

"One must be tolerant. It is difficult to demand that teachers attend in-service training programs
because it would require them to sacrifice their extra jobs.... Work discipline is lost."

– School director, poor district in Lima

On declining quality:

"The education of teachers has deteriorated. Private ISPs are responsible for the proliferation of
bad teachers since they never fail student.... The teaching title is easy to get. Anyone can be a
teacher. It's all a business."

– Director, urban marginal school in Lima

"Quality has been deteriorating over the last 15 years as a result of the proliferation of medical
faculties.... We have had to modify our recertification requirements because university degrees
cannot be trusted. The best students don't enter government service...."

– Dean, Colegio Médico del Perú, Lima

On corruption:

"We are in the hands of a mafia. Producing teaching certificates is a mass-production industry.
Universities accept students without entry examinations. Ninety percent of the teachers are
dedicated to profiteering. Grades are sold. School directors charge the most. Illegal business is
the culture due to the low wages. Teachers collude with doctors to get sickness
certificates.... Corruption has increased. To get certified, private schools pay US$5,000."

– Director of Education, regional government

"Quality has fallen over the last five years. Recruitment is corrupt. There is no evaluation of per-
sonality—some doctors are psychotics."

– A doctor at an NGO

On cultural bias:

"Many teachers have difficulties in teaching poor children. They have a cultural prejudice, be-
lieving that poor children do not have the capacity to learn. These teachers rationalize in this
way their own lack of capacity to reach those children."

– Dean of education faculty

Sources: Information in this box is based on the study of human resources in public health and education
done as part of the project. Education and health professionals, union representatives, and development
experts participated in consultations and focus group interviews. All fieldwork was done in the urban,
urban marginal, and outlying rural areas of Ayacucho, Cusco, Huamachuco, Lima, and Trujillo. Data from
opinion surveys and interviews of other existing studies were also used.

dition, without behavior change, the overall long-term impact could have damaging effects on the country's human resources. The behaviors of all actors in the social service sector are key obstacles to the delivery of better quality services: The state, including policy makers and politicians, has been unresponsive and has failed to meet its administrative or political obligations. Service users and beneficiaries are not equipped to demand high quality and good performance. Front-line providers, including teachers, doctors, nurses, and local and regional authorities, are not motivated to adopt positive change.

To address Peru's human resource challenges, RECURSO's main recommendations focused on three critical interventions: (1) setting quality standards with monitoring mechanisms and measurable goals, (2) defining clear accountability lines for providers, and (3) investing in human resource development to create the capacity to reach these goals.

Obstacles and Challenges

The RECURSO study revealed that prevailing fears, attitudes, and practices act as barriers to increased accountability and better delivery of public services. What prevents users and clients from demanding their rights to high-quality services and from bringing public pressure to bear when those rights are not met? Why are providers, policy makers, and politicians not held accountable when they fail to fulfill their public duties? What are the obstacles to compliance and to the enforcement of sanctions when public authorities deliver inadequate services, especially to the poor? The study revealed the following important findings about the obstacles confronting efforts to improve social services.

Fear of Evaluation

In Peru, there is a pervasive fear of being evaluated and of failing to meet expectations. Evaluation requires an examination of how well education and health professionals perform their work. The examination assesses both strengths and weaknesses, success and failure. Teachers and doctors, demoralized by low wages and a lack of incentive to provide high-quality services, are likely to fail such examinations and are unlikely to meet established performance standards. Their fear of such failure prompts their resistance to any system of evaluation. Moreover, an increasingly negative attitude toward performance evaluation and measurement within the education system has prompted teachers to view evaluation as intellectually suspect, nonmodern, regressive, or inequality inducing.

Resistance to Standards

Corporations and service providers oppose efforts to set clear benchmarks for measuring quality and performance. In education, teachers and school officials oppose standards, thereby effectively escaping all pressure to perform according to a set of objective criteria. Not all schools use standards; and where they exist,

---

Box 4.2. Defining Performance Standards

According to the official guidelines of the Fe y Alegría network of schools, a second-grade student should be able to

"...construct the comprehension of the text being read by anticipating the type of text and the purpose of the writing, according to context ... formulate hypotheses about the meaning of text, test his or her hypotheses against those of classmates, and draw conclusions."

"...read audibly, respecting exclamation and question marks and without sounding out syllables."

---

they are applied arbitrarily. In some cases, the lack of updated records on career-service education officials undermines the efforts to evaluate their performance. As one Ministry of Education official noted, it is essential to evaluate teachers. However, the instruments to do so are nonexistent. In particular, 80 percent of the information on the personnel files and career records of teachers has been lost. As a result, it is impossible to get any information regarding level of education attained, degrees, specializations, years of service, history of positions held (not even the last two), or on-the-job training received for all teachers.

Where standards are defined, they typically fail the test of clarity (see box 4.2). Because ambiguous, complex, and practically incomprehensible standards prevent objective evaluation, dysfunctional service delivery persists, with uninformed users left at the mercy of unaccountable service providers.

Lack of Client Information

Social service clients and users who don't know what they have a right to expect and demand, and what they are responsible for, are obstacles to a service delivery system that is functioning well. In education, the lack of transparency prevents parents from making informed choices of schools for their children. The study revealed that a school's assessment results usually are not disclosed so parents are unable to compare the quality of schools. Although both the RECURSO survey and a 2001 national assessment revealed that 80–90 percent of parents were happy with their schools, most parents also were unaware of the poor quality of learning.

In health care, the lack of reliable information about maternal and infant mortality makes it difficult to assess the quality of health service delivery. Consumers have no means to express their personal preferences and most urgent needs. In social assistance, unclear coverage and eligibility criteria lead to weak monitoring of targeted social programs. Poor information flows prevent effective tracking of progress to ensure that food programs improve children's nutritional status.

Role of Strategic Communication

The RECURSO project clearly recognized that no change is possible without alterations in behavior. The lack of accountability and the poor quality of services will persist in an environment where consumers are unaware of their rights as users, where service providers are not subject to performance standards, and where the state fails to protect user rights and sanction negligent service providers. Addressing accountability issues from a behavioral change perspective calls for an effective, well-designed communication strategy that goes beyond the simple dissemination of information.

Informing and Educating the Client

Given the right information and education, the social services' user can be an influential force in driving the cultural change called for in the RECURSO study. Increased awareness of user rights and the need for standards can create a shift in consumer attitude and can reorient public demand for quality. In education, parents' awareness is crucial in ensuring that performance standards are set to determine if the quality of instruction is low or high and if their children's learning achievements fall short or exceed established expectations. Armed with this knowledge, parents can monitor their children's progress and become active guardians during the critical early years of learning. The results of national assessments and school evaluations should be accessible to all parents because informed parents are better able to make wise decisions about schooling.

As to health care, information about eligibility criteria for health insurance coverage and about the rights of potential beneficiaries to make use of social programs will ensure that deserving households benefit from services designed to help them. Inclusive participation, especially among poor and marginalized communities, will correct information asymmetries and reduce Peru's social inequality. One of RECURSO's recommendations was to conduct systematic, native-language communication campaigns using local media and community radio and holding capacity-building activities to increase the participation of poor people. When consumers are educated about existing services and their rights to receive them, they can demand that policy makers and service providers respect their rights as citizens and provide the benefits to which they are entitled.

Strengthening Client Voice to Improve Quality

Access to information is essential but not necessarily sufficient. Transparency increases where information is available, and knowledge strengthens the user's position as a client and service beneficiary. Clients who know their rights and understand the established quality standards are important in ensuring that service providers meet their obligations. But when delivery fails, quality is undercut, and service becomes dysfunctional, informed users should have the voice and visibility to call attention to failure, provide feedback, and express dissatisfaction with state of services and service delivery.

Strategic communication can open avenues for information exchange and can identify mechanisms through which the three main actors (policy makers, service providers, and citizens/clients) can engage in free and productive debate on issues affecting quality service provision. The RECURSO study found equal numbers of opportunities in and obstacles to improving accountability and strengthening citizen voice in Peru's social service sector. Several participatory organizations exist, but they are subject to capture by service providers. For example, the national parent-teacher association is closely aligned with the teachers' union; the head of the parents' association is both a teacher and a unionist.

In social assistance programs, although community-based organizations both select the beneficiaries and deliver the food-supply services, poor households continue to have limited program access. There is also a clear lack of collective force among users. The parents' associations at the national level do not get much support from local parents' associations. Even the private sector, which has an important role to play in service delivery, is not involved in public policy debates on education.

Empowered users can be effective catalysts for change. Strategic communication carefully designed to produce empowered users can help create an inclusive, broadly participatory environment that includes poor and disadvantaged people. Through participants' collective voice they may exert enough leverage to influence public action.

Designing RECURSO's Communication Strategy

Table 4.1 illustrates how the decision tool could have been applied in the preparation of a communication strategy for the RECURSO project.

Understanding and Targeting Audiences. Using the accountability framework as the starting point in analyzing existing challenges in Peru's social sector, the RECURSO project team identified three key actors—the clients (users and the general public), the service providers (corporations and front-line professionals), and the state (policy makers, legislators, and implementers). These key actors represent specific audience segments. Further disaggregation within each of these broad groups may be necessary to develop audience-specific communication approaches. The primary audience comprises those people or institutions/agencies whose behavior most needs to be influenced. It is important to examine the knowledge, beliefs, values, and perceptions of the primary audience (the main catalysts of change) because those are the key predictors of their behavior. An in-depth understanding of those factors reached through formative research is essential in designing an effective communication strategy. The secondary audiences are equally important because they are allied closely with and can exert strong influence on the primary audience.

Table 4.1. Decision Tool: Peru's RECURSO Project

Management Objectives:
- To educate parents, community leaders, and politicians on simple and transparent standards to measure quality of children's education
- To enhance parents' ability to demand quality from teachers and school administrators
- To encourage political leaders to support simple metrics nationwide

| Audience | Behaviors | Messages | | Channels | Evaluation |
		Takeaway Message	Supporting Data		
Parents	• Test their child's reading speed (60 words in 60 seconds) to measure quality of education received • Voice concern regarding low quality of education with teachers and school administrators	• "If my second-grader can read 60 words in 60 seconds, I am assured my child is getting a good-quality education. If not, I can demand that public school teachers and administrators improve the quality of education given."	• Messages from national government leaders (presidential candidates), community leaders, and media demonstrating that children from all over Peru are able to attain recommended reading speed	• Community gatherings • Radio programs and local newspapers	• Number of parents using standard of reading speed (60 words in 60 seconds) in testing the quality of their children's education
Teachers	• Apply standard of reading speed (60 words in 60 seconds for second-graders) to assess quality of education • Improve teaching methods to enable children to increase reading speed	• "The quality of education is as important as the quantity; I will use the standard of reading speed to assess the quality of education I provide to children."	• RECURSO Project video demonstrating that children across ethnic groups and in different regions of the country are able to attain recommended reading speed • Data from national education associations, leading educators	• Radio programs, local newspapers, and RECURSO Project brochures and video	• Number of teachers using the standard of reading speed to assess the quality of education • Number of teachers receiving awards for showing the best results in reading among children in indigenous, rural, multigrade schools

| School administrators | • Enforce discipline among teachers (number of hours worked in teaching versus "second" job)
• Improve instructional methods
• Increase the quality of entrants into the teaching profession to enable students to learn to read at recommended levels
• Enhance the teaching skills of its teachers | • "If I increase the quality of education in my school (measured in terms of reading speed), my school will be recognized as a quality institution within this community (and perhaps nationally) through the annual award to the 100 best teachers in Peru." | • Annual award to 100 best teachers | • Radio programs, local newspapers, and RECURSO Project brochures and video
• National/regional meetings among school administrators | • Number of school administrators whose schools demonstrate increased quality (measured in terms of achievement of recommended reading speed)
• Number of schools with a teacher recognized as one of the 100 best teachers |
| National politicians | • Inform constituencies about Peru's problem of low-quality education
• Persuade constituents of the need to improve the quality of education
• Encourage parents to use the simple measure of reading speed to motivate community leaders, school administrators, and teachers to improve the quality of education and use reading speed as a measure of quality | • "I believe the poor quality of education hampers Peru's development. I will encourage parents, teachers, school administrators, and community leaders to use the metric of reading speed to measure education quality, to assess it regularly, and to track improvement." | • Analytical work of the RECURSO Project
• Positive media coverage of national politicians' efforts to promote reform to improve the quality of education, as embodied in the RECURSO project | • Radio, TV programs
• Formal, technical discussions with national and international educators | • Number, frequency, and reach of messages on issue politicians give to various groups |

Source: Authors' compilation.

Identifying Behaviors. Part of understanding an audience is identifying which of its behaviors act as barriers to change. In education, the RECURSO study found that users, unions, and public administrators have no incentive to reverse the declining quality of service. They have benefited from increased service coverage and continue to enjoy the power leadership and legitimacy that their positions imply. Teachers are unmotivated to perform well because of the pressure of having several jobs. Low wages and the lack of strict performance evaluations have encouraged these behaviors that negatively affect the quality of their work as educators. Parents, however, are unaware of their children's poor learning outcomes and most of them are completely satisfied by the added benefit of some free time while their children are in school. Descriptions of attitudes and circumstances, such as those presented in box 4.1, help explain what specific audiences know and believe, what influences their perceptions, and what drives them to act as they do. These descriptions help reveal the potential barriers to behavior change and the benefits that will motivate audiences to adopt new behaviors.

Framing Messages. Messages, like behaviors, should be considered audience specific. This involves framing messages that resonate with key target audiences. More important than any particular message is the audience's response to the message received, that is, their "takeaway message." What they do with the message, how they process its information, and how they respond to it will determine the success or failure of any communication effort. In Peru, the research done for the RECURSO project and other existing studies can provide the empirical basis for message content. Which messages will drive policy makers and politicians to develop standards and enforce laws and regulations that improve accountability? Which messages will encourage front-line providers, such as teachers and nurses, to give dedicated and uncompromised service to their clients, without fear of evaluation? Which messages will users and clients find compelling enough to make them demand better services? Designers of strategic communication must answer those questions if they hope to craft powerful takeaway messages that raise awareness and motivate key audiences to adopt the positive behaviors that will break the low-level equilibrium in Peru.

Selecting Effective Channels of Communication. The medium is just as important as the message. The right message conveyed through an inappropriate channel or information source may be detrimental to the overall objective of influencing behavior change. Will electronic media, with its broader reach and frequency, be more effective in convincing specific audiences about the benefits of setting standards? Or will it be more effective to use the print media and interpersonal communication in sharing information and educating the public? Audience characteristics and specific local conditions determine which channels have the greatest reach and effect in promoting new behaviors. RECURSO recommended systematic, native-language communication campaigns, the use of local media and community radio, and capacity building to increase poor people's participation in improving the social service sector. Carefully selecting the right mix of channels is necessary to communicate messages effectively to key target audiences.

Evaluating Outcomes. Progress, completion, and outcome benchmarks are an essential part of an effective communication strategy. How will communication activities be monitored and evaluated? What critical indicators will track changes in knowledge, attitudes, beliefs, and practices? If behavior changes occur, what communication support will be necessary to sustain the new behavior?

The experience in RECURSO shows positive changes since the launch of the project in 2005. President Garcia announced that his government would introduce universal testing for second-grade students, a key recommendation of RECURSO. In his speeches, President Garcia sends a message to mothers to "become aware of how many words per minute their children were able to read." Universal testing of students began in 2006 and is now an annual policy. By 2008, feedback was provided to all schools and parents. Congress passed new legislation to provide pay incentives to teachers who approve evaluations. And the Ministry of Health approved a new technical norm that includes the nutrition standards as an important element in the health communication package (Cotlear 2008).

Notes

1. Following Fujimori's 1990 election, in 1992 he abolished Congress and the regional governments and pushed for a new Constitution. Signed in 1993, the new Constitution established a unicameral Congress and centralized decision-making power within the executive branch. Channels for citizen representation were abolished in the process.
2. Data sources would include quantitative surveys and qualitative information gathered from individual interviews and focus groups with key respondents, including parents; children; teachers; nurses; doctors; and municipal, regional, and ministerial authorities in different areas of the country.
3. In Latin America, the accountability framework first was applied from a regional perspective by Fiszbein (2005). Going beyond traditional analysis of the structure and patterns of public spending, the framework focuses on the critical dimension of institutions and the relationships among three key agents or actors: (1) the individuals or clients; (2) the corporation or organization, including front-line providers and local and regional authorities; and (3) the state, including policy makers and politicians from all levels of government.
4. School enrollment levels in Peru surpass many other countries in the region, including those with higher incomes per capita; and completion rates at the primary and secondary levels are high.
5. These results of the RECURSO study of early reading development were considered disturbing despite the study's small sample of 250 children and a bias on the poorest 40 percent of the population.

6. On the basis of international standards, such as the Program for International Student Assessment, learning assessments indicate that Peru scored lower (327) on the combined reading scale than did the other countries of Latin American (411).
7. Learning inequality is measured as the ratio of performance at the 95th percentile compared with that at the 5th percentile.

References

Cotlear, Daniel, ed. 2006. *A New Social Contract for Peru: An Agenda for Improving Education, Health Care, and the Social Safety Net.* Washington, DC: World Bank.

———. 2008. "PERU: Making Accountability Work—Lessons from RECURSO." *En Breve* 135 (September): 1–4.

Fiszbein, Ariel. 2005. *Citizens, Politicians and Providers: The Latin American Experience with Service Delivery Reform.* Washington, DC: World Bank.

World Bank. 2003. *World Development Report 2004: Making Services Work for Poor People.* Washington, DC: World Bank.

The Country Assistance Strategy for the Philippines

Despite the country's tremendous growth potential, economic and political challenges continue to hamper the Philippines' ability to achieve solid and sustained progress. Struggling under a weak macroeconomic environment following the Asian financial crises in 1997, the government accumulated substantial debt. Poor tax collection, huge losses in the power sector, contingent claims on government, and bailouts of government-owned corporations drove the accumulation of debt. Moreover, the fragile fiscal situation affected public investment in social services and led to their deterioration. Since 1997, real per capita public spending has fallen by 43 percent in health care and 19 percent in education (World Bank 2005, p. 10). Social spending decreases have significant implications for the well-being of the population, 26 percent of which already lives below the poverty line in 2003 (p. 7). Weak public service delivery, infrastructure deficiencies, regulatory constraints, and a pervasive concern about corruption have resulted in a poor investment climate and the public's loss of trust in government.

Although the country's economic performance has improved since 2001, it continues to trail behind its East Asian neighbors. In 2002–03, the Philippine economy grew at an average rate of 4.5 percent, and the rate rose to 6.1 percent in 2004. Real GDP per worker indicates, however, that labor productivity increased by only 1.0 percent from 1961 to 2003, compared with an average 4.4 percent increase in other major East Asian economies. A competitiveness ranking of East Asian economies showed deterioration in the Philippines' position, while the positions of Malaysia and Thailand improved. Loss of investor confidence and a poor investment climate have been exacerbated by infrastructure deficiencies in the Philippines. Only 21 percent of the country's roads are paved, compared with 46 percent in Indonesia, 76 percent in Malaysia, and 97 percent in Thailand. School enrollment rates have increased in recent years, but the country ranked poorest in student performance on mathematics and science tests, lagging behind other East Asian countries (World Bank 2005).

People living below the poverty line in the Philippines have less access than the rest of the population to employment opportunities; education (particularly high-quality education); and such basic services as affordable health care, safe water, and sanitation. That lack of access further increases their vulnerability to ill health, natural disasters, and economic shocks. Poverty remains a problem predominantly in the rural areas, where two out of three households depend on income from agriculture. Income inequality is stark, with poor people accounting for only 6 percent of national income, whereas the wealthiest 5 percent of households account for about 30 percent of national income (World Bank 2005).

Program Profile

The World Bank, as a financial and development institution, has a long history of partnership with the Philippines. Consistent with the government's development goals and the World Bank's assessment of strategic priorities, country assistance to the Philippines has evolved from economic recovery to poverty alleviation over the last 15 years (World Bank 1999). The country assistance strategies (CASs) of 1999 and 2002 reflected an emphasis on poverty, a redefined rural strategy and program, the inclusion of judicial reform, and an enhanced partnership with civil society. The fiscal 2003–05 CAS period supported key development objectives aimed at (1) macroeconomic stability and equitable growth based on free enterprise, (2) environmentally sustainable rural development with social equity, (3) comprehensive human development through access to basic services, and (4) good and effective governance. The CAS Completion Report for fiscal 2003–05 (World Bank 2002) and the Operations Evaluation Department Review (World Bank 1999) noted acceptable progress in achieving the CAS objectives, and rated the outcome of the Bank's assistance as moderately satisfactory.

To ensure a more results-focused CAS, the World Bank's strategic approach involved the integration of key lessons from earlier country experience, particularly from a client survey and the CAS Completion Report, as well as insights gained from systematic stakeholder consultations involving key sectors of civil society.[1]

Notwithstanding improved economic performance with higher growth rates, major challenges remain. The World Bank's assessment indicates that weak public institutions are the major obstacle to the meaningful and sustainable growth necessary to benefit broader segments of society, especially the poor.

Figure 5.1. CAS Engagement Strategy

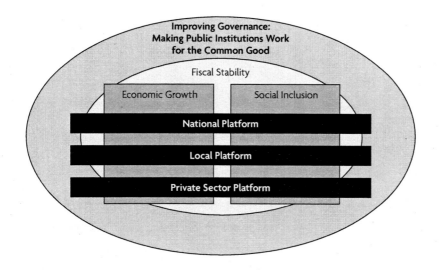

Source: World Bank 2005.

Fundamental institutional weaknesses arise from deep-rooted problems of poor governance, corruption, and a public decision-making process that favors narrow vested interests. Thus, the CAS for fiscal year 2006–08, which builds on the government's Medium-Term Development Plan, focuses on the two main goals of economic growth and social inclusion, firmly hinged on two levers for reform—namely, fiscal stability and improved governance (figure 5.1). Strategic action was pursued through three levels of intervention: (1) at the national level, through sectorwide, programmatic operations to support fiscal and governance objectives; (2) at the local level, through an integrated, cross-sectoral focus aimed at improved service delivery and increased capacity of local government units; and (3) at the private sector level, through policy and administrative improvements to eliminate bottlenecks and attract private sector investments.

Obstacles and Opportunities

The preparation of the fiscal 2006–08 CAS coincided with significant political and social developments in the Philippines—a recently elected president, a newly appointed administration, new members of Congress, and an increasingly frustrated civil society clamoring for meaningful changes. Strong negative perceptions and widespread public attention revealed key development obstacles requiring urgent and decisive action. Various assessment surveys and analytical and diagnostic efforts confirmed a pervasive negative attitude toward government and a pessimistic public view of development prospects. The following facts were noted in the fiscal 2006–08 CAS:

- More than 40 percent of respondents in the World Bank's Client Survey believed that the country was moving in the wrong direction. Addressing the problem of corruption will determine whether development progress can be achieved.
- Citizens believe that they do not receive the services they deserve and therefore question the right of government to collect taxes for inefficient or inadequate delivery of public goods and services.
- People are reluctant to support government's efforts to raise tax revenues because of their general mistrust of government and its perceived misuse of public funds.
- Many Filipinos—especially those who are poor—are highly skeptical about economic reforms and the likelihood that they will benefit from economic growth.
- Within the business community, private firms believe that the most serious constraints to investment are macroeconomic instability, corruption, regulatory policy uncertainty, crime, theft and disorder, tax rates and tax administration, and infrastructure deficiencies (particularly electricity and transport).[2]
- The youth expressed pessimism about their own futures and raised serious concerns about the problems of substance abuse, reproductive health, education, and employment opportunities.

The public's beliefs about persistent problems of graft and corruption, as well as their own experiences with poor delivery of basic services, affected their attitudes toward government. This perception prompted negative behavior among legislators and the general public, thereby adversely affecting government's efforts to raise much-needed revenues.[3] Nonpayment of taxes by a great majority of citizens and the unwillingness of legislators to approve tax increases and tariff adjustments in the power and water sectors led to further pressure on an already fragile fiscal environment.[4]

The CAS Preparation Process

Following the internal launch of the CAS preparation in July 2004, meetings with key opinion leaders and a government advisory team were held to discuss the central elements of the CAS and the process of stakeholder consultations.[5] Indeed, it was an opportune time to engage in broad outreach and dialogue to gather the public's views and identify crucial development issues. Government also saw the benefit of using the consultations to present a draft of its Medium-Term Development Plan to a broader audience. At the same time, the consultation process presented two key challenges: (1) the new government, having just assumed leadership, was reluctant to engage immediately in public dialogue; and (2) the cross-sectoral and thematic approach of the CAS presented difficult choices in managing the consultation process. For consultations to be meaningful both to the World Bank and to key stakeholders, a balance had to be struck between ensuring the quality of participation and engaging a wide and diverse set of participants; between focusing on advocacy objectives and addressing operational issues; and, in terms of geographic representation, between urban capitals or island provinces as appropriate venues for consultations.

The CAS preparation process for fiscal 2006–08 used four important building blocks as a foundation: (1) the CAS Completion Report, (2) the Client Survey, (3) results from past CAS consultations, and (4) additional stakeholder feedback. All of this input informed the policy dialogue and revealed the public's view of the most critical development concerns.

Role of Strategic Communication

Setting the groundwork for an informed public dialogue involved developing a two-way process of effective communication. This included strategic sharing of information through informal meetings with key opinion leaders, raising public awareness, engaging in productive debate through broad consultations, and providing stakeholders with feedback to keep them informed of developments and the results of the consultations. The approach fostered greater upstream communication through the gathering of input from various sectors of civil society. Table 5.1 shows the result of using the decision tool to design the communication strategy for the CAS preparation process.

Outreach and Public Communication

Systematic stakeholder consultations were designed to serve as the principal mechanism for the strategic sharing of information among the government, civil society, and the donor community. The main objective of the consultations was to solicit the views of various sectors of civil society, involving (1) key stakeholders and the general public, to obtain their views on economic problems and on the policy options and programs needed to support successful medium-term development outcomes; and (2) the World Bank's development partners and clients, to gain their input on how the Bank could improve its program of assistance and operations in the country.

To ensure a meaningful public dialogue, particular attention was given to the following considerations: (1) making the consultation process transparent, participatory, inclusive, and meaningful; (2) managing public expectations and making it clear that the process was not meant to build consensus, but rather to gain a better understanding of citizens' perspectives on issues and policy directions; and (3) organizing thematic and results-oriented multistakeholder consultations consistent with the CAS themes of growth, social inclusion, fiscal stability, and governance to help shape and confirm the focus of the World Bank's proposed CAS program.

Table 5.1. Decision Tool: Philippines CAS, FY 2006–08

Management Objectives:

- To guide CAS formulation and enhance country ownership through broad stakeholder engagement and articulation of views on key issues, policy options, and priority programs, particularly among (1) national agencies (executive, legislative, and judicial) to strengthen intragovernment collaboration and support cross-sectoral program priorities; (2) LGUs to support decentralization and increase their involvement as revenue-generating and decision-making units accountable for effective delivery of local public services; (3) the private sector and business community to help define priorities in creating an enabling environment to build investor confidence and assist government in poverty reduction programs; (4) civil society (academe, labor groups, youth groups, and NGOs) to support their roles as key sources of information on emerging issues and public sentiment and as watchdogs helping monitor the progress of CAS implementation; and (5) the donor community and development partners to ensure better coordination and harmonization of efforts and successful attainment of CAS outcomes

Audience	Behaviors	Messages		Channels	Evaluation
		Takeaway Message	Supporting Data		
National government	• Initiate an extensive and inclusive public consultation process to solicit views and identify key issues • Recognize the benefits of the upstream involvement of civil society in the CAS process	• "The government is committed to hearing the views of stakeholders, partners, and civil society groups on key development issues and policy options. Regular feedback is needed to validate inputs, manage expectations, and foster continuous public dialogue."	• Client survey • CAS completion report	• Meetings and consultations • Briefings • Seminars and workshops	• Broad consultation with various constituencies resulting in identification of critical concerns about development
Legislature	• Gain deeper understanding of and articulate views on key issues and priorities, assess their legislative implications, and propose/support relevant laws	• "Issuance of relevant bills is critical in achieving the country's development objectives."	• CAS consultation reports • Technical studies	• Newsletters • CAS Web site	• Number of legislative proposals submitted • Relevance of the legislation proposed to the critical concerns of constituencies
LGUs	• Participate actively in CAS consultations, validate issues affecting LGUs, and identify local development priorities	• "Local government units play a central role in defining the country's strategic development agenda. Active engagement in the CAS formulation will enhance ownership of policies and priorities affecting local communities."	• CAS consultation reports • Technical studies	• Newsletters • CAS Web site	• Number of LGUs participating in CAS consultations and validating critical concerns

Stakeholder group	Actions	Statements			Indicators
Private sector/business community	• Collaborate closely with government in the CAS formulation process and contribute to the articulation of issues and policy options to help stimulate private sector activity • Foster trust and confidence in government through active engagement in government-initiated development forums and public dialogue	• "Strong public-private partnerships are essential to promote economic growth and improve the investment climate. I will support the CAS formulation process through ideas and input to mobilize private sector participation." • "The government is committed to support the private sector as key development partners."	• Client survey • CAS completion report	• Roundtable discussions • Briefings and seminars • Discussion forums	• Number of private sector groups participating in the CAS process and advocating the need for government action on critical barriers to development
Civil society organizations: • academic community • labor groups • youth groups • NGOs	• Engage in constructive and open dialogue • Present objective views on important issues and policy options for consideration in the CAS process	• *For supporters:* "We strongly support the CAS consultation process and will continue to monitor issues and give feedback to the government on issues of concern." • *For opponents:* "We will participate in this consultation as advocates of change. We are aware of the difficult environment and the government's constraints in addressing the country's macroeconomic, social, and political challenges. It is a welcome opportunity to have our voices heard and our views considered in policy deliberations." • *For uncommitted and involved parties:* "We see the importance of the consultation process as a venue for expressing our concerns. Convinced of the benefits of active engagement, we will support broad civil society participation."	• CAS consultation reports	• CAS Web site	• Number of civil society organizations engaged in discussion and debate of CAS-related issues as active participants in the CAS process • Number of key civil society organizations advocating CAS-related reforms with political leaders

Source: Authors' compilation.

Note: CAS = country assistance strategy; LGU = local government unit; NGO = nongovernmental organization.

Public Dialogue and Consultations

In keeping with the World Bank's open and participatory CAS process, a two-pronged approach was adopted in conducting the public consultations—one prong at the national level, with key representatives from the executive, legislative, and judicial branches; and the other prong at the local government level, with chief executives from two of the major islands, Visayas and Mindanao. In addition, representatives from the business community/private sector, labor groups, academia, and civil society participated in the consultation workshops.

Multistakeholder Consultations. From August to October 2004, close to 300 participants attended five consultation workshops, two in Manila and one in each of the three regional capitals. Such an approach ensured balanced geographic representation of stakeholders from the northern (Tuguegarao), central (Cebu), and southern (Davao) parts of the country. Consultations were done in partnership with the government's central planning agency, the National Economic Development Authority. The network of private and academic institutions under the umbrella of the World Bank's Knowledge for Development Centers was involved as well.[6]

Consistent with the thematic, cross-sectoral framework of the CAS, multistakeholder consultations included designated breakout sessions to discuss thematic issues on enhancing macroeconomic stability and economic growth, addressing social inclusion and equitable development, and strengthening public sector performance. In the regional consultations, discussions focused on promoting rural growth and development, reducing poverty, and improving governance at the local level. The CAS themes were drawn from the government's 10-Point Agenda and the National Development Agenda.

Focus Group Consultations. Focus groups were formed to solicit input on growth, social inclusion, and governance. The discussions provided more in-depth perspectives on specific topics from each of the following stakeholder groups:

- Congress—selected policy reforms (fiscal and public sector reforms)
- the business community and key opinion leaders—vision and broad policy agenda
- leaders of local governments—specific policy agenda concerning local government units
- the Club of 29—implementation issues concerning World Bank projects[7]
- the donor community—measures to improve donor coordination.

Levels of Communication

The highly participatory nature of the CAS preparation facilitated the various levels of communication within and across sectors of government and civil society. The joint participation of national-level executives, key legislators, and regional and local government officials in the multistakeholder meetings facil-itated intragovernmental communication. High-level local chief executives voiced their concerns, particularly on the issue of local governance, and pro-vided valuable input.

With civil society organizations and labor groups also represented in the multistakeholder consultations, discussions on the elements of the proposed CAS program of action fostered open and productive communication between government and civil society. The Philippines has a robust and vibrant civil so-ciety sector with diverse political and functional interests.[8] Given the right op-portunity and a positive environment, civil society's participation can con-tribute substantially to the policy dialogue. Discussions with this group also helped identify the need for World Bank assistance to improve the capacity of civil society organizations to engage national and local governments in plan-ning, project implementation, and monitoring.

Focus group discussions also enhanced communication among government, the donor community, and international development partners. It also provided the opportunity to define the scope for closer collaboration and continued har-monization between the World Bank's CAS and the rest of the donor commu-nity in the Philippines.

Communication Channels and the Feedback Mechanism

The CAS process is an iterative process of consultation, communication, and feed-back (Muthuram and Shah 2002). The most appropriate channels of communi-cation were used to achieve its objective of disseminating information and ob-taining the public's views on development issues and the proposed assistance program. Priority was given to interpersonal, face-to-face communication, which provided ample opportunity to engage in focused discussion of key issues through formal and informal meetings, focus group gatherings, and multistakeholder con-sultations. Personal interactions with consulted groups, although more time in-tensive than the broad reach of mass media, was effective both in communicating the CAS objectives and in building client and partner relationships.

Interpersonal communication also produced a more effective feedback process. Having distilled the findings from the consultations, World Bank staff confirmed that the feedback received validated the importance of the CAS themes. Input from each series of consultations helped refine the CAS and sharp-ened its focus to align it closely with the Philippine government's Medium-Term Development Plan. When consultations were complete, individual letters were sent to inform each participant of the results of those consultations. A Feedback Report documenting the process and its outcomes in detail was pre-pared and subsequently distributed to a wider audience.

To further promote a transparent process, public access was provided through a Web site containing updated information on the progress of the CAS consultations.

Outcomes, Lessons Learned, and Challenges Remaining

The design of systematic consultations enhanced both the process and the substance of the Philippine CAS. Increased intragovernment participation, a well-defined scope of civil society involvement, and donor coordination and feedback mechanisms ensured good-quality participation in preparing the CAS. The process also helped combine the substance of a results-based CAS with a thematic focus. Consultations helped achieve the following outcomes: (1) they validated the broad themes and critical measures that would constitute a strategic action agenda initially formulated by the World Bank, (2) they identified key players (such as actors at the national level, in local government units, and within private sector) and defined their roles in implementing the action agenda, and (3) they defined the role of the World Bank and the scope of its program of assistance in the reform process.

From a communications standpoint, the Philippines CAS incorporated the key elements in establishing good communication throughout the consultation process. Strategic information sharing and early consultation and communication were initiated in the planning stages through informal meetings with key government officials and influential opinion leaders. In designing the consultation process, the scope of public debate was defined by following the thematic approach of the CAS because it ensured a focused and productive discussion of key issues from a cross-section of Philippine civil society. Moreover, the consultation process itself was designed to facilitate active listening to stakeholder views while managing public expectations.

Summaries of the CAS consultations and the Client Survey are provided in annex B of the CAS document (World Bank 2005). They highlighted the key messages from the stakeholders and the four CAS themes—growth, social inclusion, fiscal stability, and governance. One of the most significant findings emerging from the consultations was the vital importance of addressing social inclusion and governance, two issues that garnered near-unanimous attention among stakeholders.

There remains a strong public call for bold and decisive action to address corruption and improve governance. As the fiscal 2006–08 CAS notes, "Many of the solutions are political, requiring action by the legislature" (World Bank 2005). In 2003, the Philippines enacted landmark legislation on public procurement, thus illustrating that important foundations for political action have been set. The process of passing those new laws involved building a reform coalition and using an effective communication strategy to create public awareness and push legislative action through strong advocacy for procurement reform.

Moving forward, the biggest challenge for the Philippines is implementing the CAS within a complex political environment. The program expects to deliver results by working collaboratively with government, the donor community, and civil society to build "islands of governance" in the Philippines, supported by public institutions that function effectively and efficiently. Meeting that expectation will require concerted action and continued outreach to key stakeholders, opinion leaders, and members of civil society to build public awareness and broad consensus on the challenges and opportunities the Philippines faces.

Notes

1. The CAS Completion Report reviews the World Bank Group's effectiveness over the previous five years and indicates that the Bank Group supported several key country development objectives, including expansion of basic infrastructure in rural areas, reconstruction efforts in Mindanao, and improved procurement and financial processes within several key agencies. The Client Survey assesses stakeholders' attitudes toward the Bank and the effectiveness of its work in the country and in addressing broader development issues.
2. This finding is based on an Investment Climate Assessment survey of 716 Philippine firms, conducted in 2004 by the Asian Development Bank and the World Bank.
3. Tax revenues declined from 17.0 percent of GDP in 1997 to 12.3 percent in 2004 (World Bank 1999).
4. Legislative inaction on taxation measures and tariff adjustments resulted in failure to satisfy CAS fiscal triggers and in subsequent cancellation of three large-scale development policy loans (World Bank 1999).
5. The government counterpart/advisory team consisted of senior government officials from the National Economic Development Authority, the Department of Finance, and the Department of Budget and Management.
6. These private and academic institutions included St. Paul University (Manila), the University of Southeastern Philippines (Davao City), the University of San Carlos (Cebu City), Silliman University (Dumaguete City), and the Asian Institute of Management (Makati City). In 1997, the first Knowledge for Development Center (KDC) began as the Bank's public information center. It has become a nationwide network of nine KDCs partnering with private and state universities. The centers share information through books, training, workshops, and dialogues. They engage the community in informed discussion and encourage people to get involved in development.
7. The Club of 29 comprises the directors of all World Bank–assisted projects.
8. More than 70,000 nonprofit organizations are registered in the country, and 7,000 of them are foundations or nongovernmental organizations working in development.

References

Muthuram, Vidhya, and Parmesh Shah. 2002. "Participatory Processes in the Country Assistance Strategies: Retrospective FY01." World Bank, Washington, DC. http://sitere sources.worldbank.org/INTPCENG/1143251-1116574134357/20509179/partprocess CAS2001.pdf [accessed April 10, 2009].

World Bank. 1999. *Philippines: From Crisis to Opportunity.* Country Assistance Review. Washington, DC: World Bank.

———. 2002. *Philippines: Improving the Lives of the Poor through Growth and Empowerment.* Washington, DC: World Bank.

———. 2005. "Country Assistance Strategy (CAS), Republic of the Philippines, FY 2006–2008." World Bank, Washington, DC.

6

Reforming Public Procurement in the Philippines, FY 2006–08

This chapter provides a brief description of the Philippines' experience in building an effective reform coalition to win legislative approval of the landmark Government Procurement Reform Act.[1] It also discusses the communication strategy that mobilized the media to increase public awareness and generate public action to push procurement reforms. The Philippines' experience offers valuable lessons in managing reform in a complex political environment. Indeed, although the reform process presented many challenges, the passage of the law in 2003 has opened significant opportunities for accelerating progress in addressing persistent, deep-rooted problems of corruption in the country.

Prior to the reform initiatives, the procurement system in the Philippines was governed by a proliferation of outdated, disparate, and sometimes inconsistent laws and regulations. The system, as dysfunctional as it was complex, was filled with gaps that left ample room for abuse and corrupt practices. In the Philippines, procurement is largely perceived as synonymous with corruption. Some studies have shown that four out of the top five agencies considered to be the most corrupt are involved in government contracting (Social Weather Stations 2002).

The 1998 budget reforms under the Filipino Medium-Term Expenditure Framework called attention to the fragmented system of procurement and the uncoordinated administrative responsibilities of agencies involved in the process.[2] Reform-minded leaders in government took on the formidable task of initiating change within a system long considered highly inefficient and corrupt. In particular, Benjamin Diokno, the newly appointed secretary of budget and management with administrative responsibility for supervising the government's purchases of goods and supplies, tackled the systemic problems of procurement. An all-encompassing law or an "omnibus code" was seen to be a necessary part of rationalizing the procurement system.

The Long Road to Reform

As the Philippines' experience shows, certain strategic steps were crucial in successfully managing a reform process that led to the signing of the Procurement Reform Bill (see figure 6.1). Having an in-depth understanding of problems in the procurement system and of stakeholder perceptions of reform was a necessary starting point (figure 6.2). With the support of donor assistance, diagnostic work began in August 1999. Within a six-month period, procurement consultants completed an analysis of the government's procurement system. A draft law was prepared with proposed provisions covering the purchasing of goods and supplies, contracting for civil works and with consultants, selling of assets, and privatizing through build-operate-transfer schemes to rationalize national, provincial, and local procurement (see Gobiel and Jobidon [1999]).

Winning the Executive Branch

With the diagnostic work completed and the proposed law drafted, the first roadblock reformers encountered was the lack of support within the proponent agency, the Department of Budget and Management. Unfamiliar with the internal workings of government and the sociopolitical environment, the foreign procurement reform consultants overlooked the need to promote ownership of the reform within the government's policy and technical staff. The senior and mid-level government officials and staff assigned to the project were neither motivated nor committed to take the necessary steps to move reform forward. The process ground to a halt, with no further action taken on the study or the draft law.

Committed to addressing procurement problems, Secretary Diokno put the process back on track through a budget reform process assisted by the U.S. Agency for International Development. Charged with reviving the study, the program team and the Budget Reform Task Force reworked the diagnostic process and organized a "shoot-down" workshop to review the consultants' diagnostic study and rebuild it from the ground up to create ownership. Approximately 60 government procurement experts and representatives from the donor community participated in the two-day workshop, and the event was well received.[3] The gathering served as a good venue for effectively engaging relevant stakeholders within government, tapping their expertise on procurement, and seeking feedback on the technical study.

The workshop's rigorous process of review and deliberation resulted in a report that essentially was consistent with the consultants' study and validated

Figure 6.1. Passage Timeline: Procurement Reform in the Philippines, 1998–2003

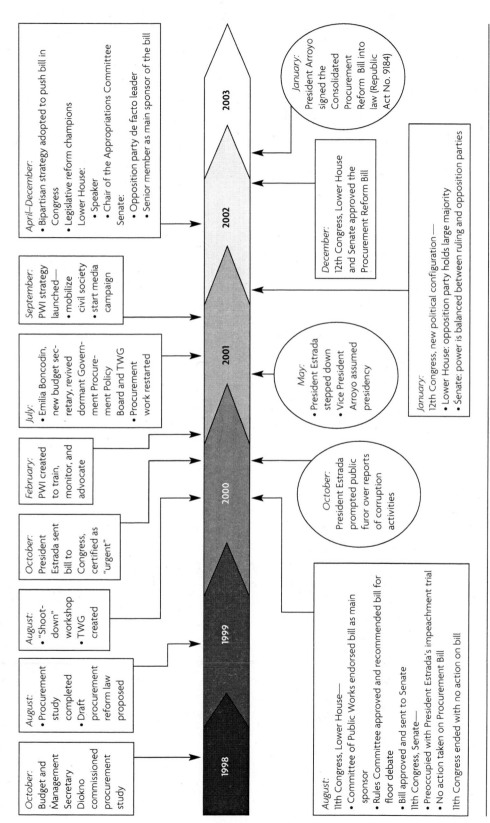

October:
Budget and Management Secretary Diokno commissioned procurement study

August:
• Procurement study completed
• Draft procurement reform law proposed

August:
• "Shoot-down" workshop
• TWG created

October:
President Estrada sent bill to Congress, certified as "urgent"

February:
PWI created to train, monitor, and advocate

July:
• Emilia Boncodin, new budget secretary, revived dormant Government Procurement Policy Board and TWG
• Procurement work restarted

September:
PWI strategy launched—
• mobilize civil society
• start media campaign

April–December:
• Bipartisan strategy adopted to push bill in Congress
• Legislative reform champions

Lower House:
  • Speaker
  • Chair of the Appropriations Committee

Senate:
  • Opposition party de facto leader
  • Senior member as main sponsor of the bill

January:
President Arroyo signed the Consolidated Procurement Reform Bill into law (Republic Act No. 9184)

December:
12th Congress, Lower House and Senate approved the Procurement Reform Bill

May:
• President Estrada stepped down
• Vice President Arroyo assumed presidency

October:
President Estrada prompted public furor over reports of corruption activities

January:
12th Congress, new political configuration—
• Lower House: opposition party holds large majority
• Senate: power is balanced between ruling and opposition parties

August:
11th Congress, Lower House—
• Committee of Public Works endorsed bill as main sponsor
• Rules Committee approved and recommended bill for floor debate
• Bill approved and sent to Senate

11th Congress, Senate—
• Preoccupied with President Estrada's impeachment trial
• No action taken on Procurement Bill

11th Congress ended with no action on bill

1998   1999   2000   2001   2002   2003

Source: Authors' illustration.
Note: PWI = Procurement Watch Inc.; TWG = technical working group.

Figure 6.2. Various Parties' Perceptions of Procurement Reform

Perception of Government Reformers (TWG)	Perception of Members of Congress from Small Towns/Districts
PROCUREMENT REFORM	**PROCUREMENT REFORM**
Omnibus Code consolidates executive orders, laws, regulations	Procurement rules apply universally across country	Lots of control over procurement system in small town	Favored companies face competition from outsiders
Ownership by executive branch will lead to passage of bill with minimum compromise	Lower costs of contracts	Increased number of bidders	Competitive advantage of local companies is not recognized
	Select best contractor for the job	"Sweetheart deals" are more difficult	
	Reduce processing time from 6–12 months to 1–3 months		
More resources for government and more effective use of those resources		Loss of contracts for favored companies	

Source: J. Edgardo Campos.
Note: TWG = technical working group.

their earlier analysis and key findings. More important, the shoot-down exercise empowered government stakeholders to lend their voices and technical expertise to the diagnostic process—and thereby develop a greater sense of ownership of the reform. The process also helped map out an action plan to implement over the succeeding three-month period. This plan involved forming a technical working group (TWG) to oversee the completion of the omnibus bill and its submission to Congress, holding regular TWG meetings and consultations, and making the TWG a participant in congressional deliberations on the omnibus bill.[4]

The three-month engagement within government had two positive outcomes: (1) it established strong relationships among the TWG members who were brought together by a shared commitment to the procurement reform initiative, and (2) it helped form a solid government position in procurement reform through regular deliberations and positive dialogue within the group. Despite the members' diverse views and different institutional perspectives, the group eventually arrived at a clear consensus and a unified stance for government. This union signaled the legislature that the reform initiative had the strong and solid backing of all relevant government agencies. Such a message was vital in assuring legislators that the draft law had been subjected to thorough and rigorous technical review and could withstand the test of legislative debate. Similarly, the unified stance made it clear to unconvinced or opposing legislators that they would face difficulty in tearing down the reform initiative because the full contingent of committed government stakeholders stood in favor of pursuing meaningful changes in the country's procurement system.

Lobbying Within the Legislature

Clearing the legislative hurdle presented several challenges to the government's reform leaders. First, strong opposition was expected among legislators who had personal vested interests in maintaining the existing procurement system, and the opposition had to be addressed. Attempting to clean up the system always had been a politically contentious issue. Introducing sweeping changes to enhance fairness, transparency, and accountability posed an obvious danger to those members of Congress who reaped personal gains from kickbacks, commissions, or contracts awarded to constituents with vested interests. Second, unwavering support from potential sponsors in the Lower House and Senate and from other allies had to be ensured. Supportive legislators, especially those who were willing to sponsor the bill, had to be convinced of the political benefits of associating themselves with a highly controversial piece of legislation. Third, the proposed bill went through the legislative mill twice. During the 11th Congress, the bill received Lower House approval, but failed to get the Senate's attention because that body was intensely focused on the impeachment trial of President Joseph Estrada in response to charges of corruption. After Estrada stepped down and his vice president, Gloria Macapagal-Arroyo, took over as president, the Procurement Reform Bill was taken up again by Congress. Committed to good governance and to an anticorruption agenda, the new president declared passage of the Procurement Reform Bill an important priority for her administration.

Successfully navigating the legislative network in both rounds demanded strategic planning and several one-on-one consultations and negotiations with legislators and their technical staffs. Securing approval of the bill required (1) identifying the appropriate legislative committee to approach, (2) finding a credible and influential member willing to sponsor the bill, and (3) scheduling the bill for legislative debate at an appropriate time in the legislative calendar.

Mobilizing Legislative Champions in the 11th Congress. Given the task of identifying the appropriate committee to approach for support of the reform bill, the legislative liaison office of the Department of Budget and Management approached the Public Works Committee and Congressman Neptali M. Gonzalez II, an influential member of the committee who had filed an earlier bill on sanctions for violations of government contracting regulations. Gonzalez later agreed to sponsor the bill. Recognizing the importance of legislative measures on anticorruption, the committee approved the bill with no amendments and submitted it for congressional floor debate. In the meantime, strong public sentiment was growing against President Estrada, and there were calls for his impeachment. The Lower House of Congress was putting the impeachment process in motion and filed an impeachment request with the Senate as the body empowered under the Constitution to handle impeachment proceedings.

The 11th Congress had two weeks left before its scheduled recess when Gonzalez took on sponsorship of the bill, and the likelihood of getting the procurement bill on the debate calendar was very slim. Congressman Gonzalez, however, was also an influential member of the Rules Committee, which had jurisdiction over the debate timetable. He skillfully managed to get the bill included in the regular schedule of debates. The timing of the bill presentation was a strategic tactic because it was done during a quorum when most of the expected opponents were not present. An overwhelming majority approved the bill, and 36 Lower House members served as cosponsors.

The next hurdle was gaining the approval of the Senate. The reform team successfully approached the Senate Committee on Constitutional Rules and Amendments and got the agreement of the majority floor leader to cosponsor the bill with the committee's chair. However, with the Senate focused on the presidential impeachment trial and the elections only five months away, the bill eventually was lost in the shuffle and failed to secure Senate approval.

Creating Bipartisan Ownership in the 12th Congress. Congress resumed with a new political configuration that called for a bipartisan legislative strategy to move the Procurement Reform Bill forward. In the Lower House, where the ruling party had a majority, reformers approached their influential legislators. Both Speaker of the Lower House Jose de Venecia and Congressman Rolando Andaya Jr., chair of the Appropriations Committee, agreed to cosponsor the bill.

To secure ownership within his legislative staff, Congressman Andaya requested the creation of a congressional technical working group comprising the TWG, selected members of the Appropriations Committee, and Procurement Watch Inc. (PWI) as a civil society representative. Several meetings of the group provided the legislative staff and the congressman with a deeper understanding of the issues, developed trust among the group members, and facilitated informal negotiations with key legislators—all of which contributed to gaining the committee's approval. Two key provisions were introduced as amendments to the bill, giving preference to domestic firms in the procurement of goods and granting preference to local provincial contractors for priority projects. After five months, an overwhelming majority of the Lower House passed the bill for Senate approval in October 2002.

The strategy for winning the Senate was bipartisan and involved approaching an influential member from the opposition party to sponsor the bill. Unlike the

Lower House, the Senate had a more balanced distribution of party affiliations, so a sponsor from the opposition party was more likely to sway the opposition to vote in favor of the bill. After several presentations and discussions with the budget secretary and the reform coalition, Senator Edgardo Angara, an influential legislator and the opposition's spokesperson, agreed to act as sponsor. A Senate TWG with representatives from both parties and from the government and civil society reform team drafted the Senate version of the bill. After six months of technical working group meetings, committee presentations, and informal gatherings to secure broad support from Upper House members, the Senate passed its version of the bill. The Senate bill was almost identical to the government's version but excluded the Lower House's two amendments.

In December 2002, the Bicameral Conference Committee convened to review the two versions and prepared a consolidated bill. The Senate and the Lower House approved the Consolidated Procurement Reform Bill, and President Macapagal-Arroyo then signed it. The reform was enacted as Republic Act No. 9184 in January 2003.

Grounding the Reform Process on Three Solid Pillars

Passing the reform bill took more than three years of painstaking work by committed reform leaders and supporters within government, the legislature, the business community, and civil society (figure 6.1). As a complex and politically charged issue, streamlining the procurement system required careful planning and strategic decision making, firmly grounded on sound technical analysis. The diagnostic work, a critical input in the process, provided a solid assessment of procurement problems that helped in crafting firm and convincing arguments for legislative debate. It also identified potential obstacles and pitfalls that could jeopardize the process. Armed with such valuable knowledge, the reform group pursued action in three key areas to minimize the risk of opposition and increase the chances for success in securing legislative approval of the reform bill.

Enlisting a Solid Core of Reform Champions. Experience has shown that making the case for reform is more effective with the active involvement of "champions" who strongly endorse the reform agenda and serve as respected and credible messengers. In the Philippines' experience, enlisting champions in both the executive and legislative branches greatly influenced broad stakeholder support. Within government, the close and continued collaboration of the government working groups helped build a reliable core of reform champions. Even with the change in political leadership, the core reform group remained intact. Members' steadfast involvement provided much-needed continuity and sustained the process through a period of uncertainty and political turmoil.

Engaging Broad Sectors of Civil Society. Just as the government reform group had evolved into a cohesive unit after several months of working together, its members realized that civil society was a critical missing link. PWI was established in February 2001, with support from the World Bank–managed ASEM Trust Fund, to promote transparency and accountability in government procurement through research, partnerships, training, and advocacy. PWI was created by a group of concerned citizens from government, academia, the legal profession, and the private sector, who shared a commitment to supporting the government's anticorruption efforts. To build public support for the passage of the reform bill, PWI focused on securing buy-in from key civil society groups and on working with the media to maintain heightened public awareness of corruption in government procurement and of the need for urgent executive and legislative action to counter it.

Various civil society groups representing the different key stakeholders were mobilized to support the proposed reform legislation. Group meetings, presentations, and training workshops were held to inform and educate the various audiences on the issues and the proposed reform. Letters of endorsement from and manifestos declaring the support of the following influential stakeholders strengthened the position of the proposed bill during legislative deliberations: (1) the Transparency and Accountability Network, a nongovernmental organization with 20 members; (2) *Walang Ku-Corrupt* (Say No to Bribery), an anticorruption movement of 13 university student councils; (3) the Roman Catholic Bishops Conference of the Philippines; (4) Philippine Chambers of Commerce and the Philippine Contractors Association, as representatives of the private business sector[5]; and (5) the League of Governors, comprising all provincial governors in the country.

Mobilizing the Power of Communication and the Media. Developing a broad-based coalition for reform required the power of a strategically designed communication plan and the reach of the mass media (see table 6.1 and figure 6.3). To support advocacy efforts, the reform group mounted a strategic media campaign aimed at communicating clear, consistent messages in support of the proposed legislation and at explaining the benefits of procurement reform. A professional group of advertising and public relations specialists was hired to roll out a media plan that involved radio, television, and print distribution of information and promotional materials, all aimed at creating a "brand" with a distinct and memorable image (figure 6.4).

To achieve effective audience targeting, the takeaway messages delivered to unique audience segments answered for each of them the question, What's in it for me? A good understanding of the audiences' perceptions and attitudes enabled communication planners to craft messages that resonated with specific audiences. Reform champions from government and the legislature also were mobilized as credible messengers. They were given air time in television interviews and on other programs to inform the public about the benefits of the proposed bill.

Table 6.1. Decision Tool: Philippines' Procurement Reform

Management Objectives:
- To raise public awareness about the benefits of reforms in public procurement
- To generate public support for a legislative bill that will improve the procurement system and address problems of corruption
- To obtain legislative approval of the Procurement Reform Bill

Audience	Behaviors	Messages		Supporting Data	Channels	Evaluation
		Takeaway Message				
National government, executive branch	• Undertake extensive review of public procurement and present objective measures and recommendations for improving procurement system • Work collaboratively with legislative branch and broad sectors of civil society in the reform process	• "Reforming the public procurement system is a critical step in fighting corruption. Government needs to adopt a unified approach in pursuing procurement reform based on solid technical analysis." • "The government is committed to hearing the views of stakeholders, partners, and civil society groups on key development issues and policy options. Regular feedback is needed to validate input, manage expectations, and foster continuous public dialogue."		• Technical studies • Public opinion survey	• Meetings and consultations • Workshops • Training and seminars • Information materials	• Focus group • Evaluation survey
National legislature (Lower House and Senate)	• Approve legislation and legislative amendments to improve the procurement system	• "Legislators play a central role in instituting anticorruption measures. And legislative approval of the procurement bill will have far-reaching benefits to improve governance in the public sector."		• Technical studies • Public opinion survey	• Meetings and seminars • Legislative champions	• Legislative records • Focus group • Evaluation survey

(continued on next page)

Table 6.1. Decision Tool: Philippines' Procurement Reform *(continued)*

Audience	Behaviors	Messages		Channels	Evaluation
		Takeaway Message	Supporting Data		
Local government officials	• Work closely with government in defining procurement issues affecting LGUs • Ensure that key provisions on LGU procurement are covered adequately in the proposed bill • Assist in focusing public attention on the importance of the proposed bill	• "LGUs need to coordinate closely with government in its efforts to rationalize the procurement system. The need for procurement reform at the level of LGUs is essential to fully realize the objectives of the Local Government Code." • "Local government officials should strongly endorse the proposed bill to underscore the need for procurement reform at the sub-national level."	• Technical studies • Public opinion survey	• Meetings of the League of Governors, whose membership consisted of all provincial governors in the country • AM-radio talk shows that featured national and local government officials in "live" interviews about procurement reform • Two-day conference series conducted around the country over an 18-month period, sponsored by the Philippine Association of Government Budget Analysts and the Association of Government Accountants of the Philippines whose members are current and former government officials from central and local governments.	• Focus group • Evaluation survey • Minutes of meetings • Media coverage of issues and people supporting or opposing procurement reform
Civil society: • private sector/business community • anticorruption NGOs • churches • students	• Support the government's advocacy efforts to get legislative approval of the procurement bill • Assist government in clearly communicating the benefits of procurement reform to various sectors of civil society	• "The private sector and the business community will benefit greatly from good public governance. We should lead advocacy efforts to get Congress to act on the Procurement Reform Bill." • "Key sectors of civil society play a central role in strengthening the government's advocacy efforts and in supporting the successful implementation of procurement reform."	• Stakeholder consultations	• Business roundtable meetings • Conferences and public development forums • TV, radio programs • Print media • Advertising campaign (streamers, posters, stickers, and giveaways)	• Minutes of meetings • Public opinion polls • Evaluation survey • Media coverage of issues and people supporting or opposing procurement reform

Source: Authors' compilation.

Note: LGU = local government unit; NGO = nongovernmental organization.

Figure 6.3. Procurement Reform Targeting Strategies

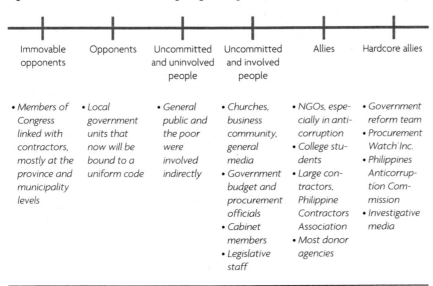

Immovable opponents	Opponents	Uncommitted and uninvolved people	Uncommitted and involved people	Allies	Hardcore allies
• Members of Congress linked with contractors, mostly at the province and municipality levels	• Local government units that now will be bound to a uniform code	• General public and the poor were involved indirectly	• Churches, business community, general media • Government budget and procurement officials • Cabinet members • Legislative staff	• NGOs, especially in anticorruption • College students • Large contractors, Philippine Contractors Association • Most donor agencies	• Government reform team • Procurement Watch Inc. • Philippines Anticorruption Commission • Investigative media

Source: J. Edgardo Campos.
Note: NGO = nongovernmental organization.

The media strategy was successful in elevating the public's attention on the issues of corruption in procurement and in generating public support for passage of the reform legislation. The success of the strategy offers some important lessons in the use of different communication channels:

- Radio—AM-frequency radio is the most popular and powerful channel of communication among lower-income and rural households in the Philippines. PWI organized an information briefing for AM-radio announcers to educate them on the need for reform and the benefits expected from the approved legislation. The announcers responded positively and conducted prime-time interviews with politicians and legislators. Equipped with a good understanding of the proposed bill, they were able to engage in productive exchanges and to send members of Congress a clear message about the importance of supporting the bill.
- Television—Because television is the medium preferred by the Philippine middle class and the intellectual elite, specific programs were targeted to reach those audience segments. Talk-show interviews were held with legislative champions and reform spokespeople, and a special documentary on the procurement reform aired on a leading cable news channel. These presentations were effective in reaching policy makers and the public and convincing them about the benefits of the proposed bill.
- Print—Public education about the consequences of corruption and the benefits of procurement reform was accomplished through regular press releases, special articles, and focused publications. To ensure accurate and informed

Figure 6.4. The Media Campaign: Communication Strategy

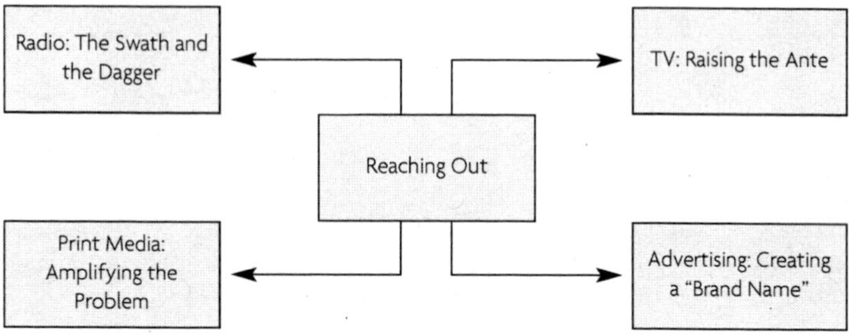

Source: J. Edgardo Campos.

reports from the print media, journalists were invited to various meetings and conferences, especially those organized by the reform group.

- Advertising—Creating a "brand" for the procurement reform initiative helped establish a positive, consistent, and memorable image for the reform process. Distributing creative promotional materials—of posters, streamers, and stickers—heightened public awareness of the procurement reform agenda and served as constant reminders of much-needed public support for anticorruption measures.

Lessons Learned

The main pillars of the reform process demonstrate that the combined impact of active civil society engagement and committed reform champions supported by an effective communication strategy effectively mobilized public action and prompted the passage of landmark legislation. Not to be overlooked, however, is the most important lesson of the Philippines' experience: the crucial presence of a cohesive core group of government reformers providing the solid foundation in the midst of a politically fragile reform environment. Working as a well-oiled machine, the reform coalition skillfully navigated the challenging political landscape and successfully led the country to procurement reform.

Notes

1. This chapter is based on information gathered from Campos and Syquia (2006). Campos is the lead public sector specialist in the Policy Reduction and Economic Management Vice Presidency at the World Bank. He served as the government's adviser for budget reforms and led the procurement reform initiative. Syquia is a professor of law at the University of Santo Tomas, Philippines.
2. Such an inefficient system largely was responsible for procurement bottlenecks, including failed bids, court-contested awards, contract disputes, serious delays in registration and

licensing of contractors and suppliers, and weaknesses in monitoring and enforcing procurement rules and regulations.

3. The government departments represented at the workshop included Budget and Management, Public Works and Highways, Education, Health, Finance, Transportation and Communications, National Economic Development Authority, the Commission on Audit, and Government Procurement Service. Also represented were members of Congress, the Economic Coordinating Council, the Office of the President, and the Flagship Programs Committee. The donor representatives included the Asian Development Bank, the United Nations Development Programme, the U.S. Agency for International Development, and the World Bank.

4. The TWG comprised representatives (with alternates) from each of the departments and agencies participating in procurement reform.

5. Mediators were key in securing the support of both groups. Convincing the Philippine Contractors Association was perceived to be more of a challenge because the personal vested interests of some members might put them in opposition to the proposed reform.

References

Campos, J. Edgardo, and Jose Luis Syquia. 2006. *Managing the Politics of Reform: Overhauling the Legal Infrastructure of Public Procurement in the Philippines.* World Bank Working Paper 70. Washington, DC: World Bank.

Gobiel, Gaetan, and Ginette Jobidon. 1999. "Review and Assessment of Procurement Systems and Procedures in the Philippines." U.S. Agency for International Development, Washington, DC.

Social Weather Stations. 2002. "Surveys of Enterprises on Public Sector Corruption." Presentation to the Asian Institute of Management, Manila, Philippines, March 21.

7

Implementing the Philippine Procurement Reform Law

This chapter presents a brief account of the ongoing implementation of procurement reform in the Philippines following passage of the Government Procurement Reform Act in 2003. Strategic communication was the glue that cemented synergistic actions taken by coalitions to support the Procurement Reform Bill as legislation was debated for three years in the executive branch and the legislature. Communication activities targeted legislators, increasing their awareness of the proposed bill, engaging them in public dialogue about its merits, and ultimately persuading them to vote for its passage. Mobilizing constituencies of support included a well-orchestrated media strategy that used AM-frequency radio to establish "live" interaction between citizens and their elected officials in the legislature; a television documentary aired on the local cable news channel to target policy makers; print media to reach urban opinion makers; and a nationwide promotional campaign to create a brand for procurement reform, with the tagline, "Stop Corruption: Move Forward with Procurement Reform."

The law—which consolidated more than 60 laws pertaining to public procurement and covered all national agencies, government-owned and -controlled corporations, government entities and instrumentalities, and local government units—institutionalized transparency measures in the competitive bidding process. Newspaper advertisements, general-circulation publications, and a procurement Web site enabled wide public dissemination of bid invitations and information about bid awards, ensuring a procurement system that was open and transparent. A Web-based government electronic procurement system became the platform for centralized government procurement and the primary source of information on all government procurement transactions. Civil society participated as observers in the bidding process conducted by the bids and awards committees of various government entities.

Building Implementation Capacity

The Philippine Department of Budget and Management created the Government Procurement Policy Board (GPPB) and charged it with responsibility for implementing the Government Procurement Reform Act of 2003. After the law was passed, government reformers focused their efforts on the implementation machinery and ramped up training and capacity-building activities. A National Training Program was designed and rolled out to equip procurement officers and staffs at various government-owned and -controlled agencies with the necessary knowledge and skills to follow the rules and regulations that guide procurement practices. The Philippine League of Budget Officers, the Commission on Audit, and the Department of Budget and Management were part of the first cohort of government officers trained, including the members of the Composite Team of Trainers. Other parallel implementation activities included developing the Government Electronic Procurement System; creating the procurement Web site; and making presentations about the new procurement law's implementation to business groups, civil society, and the media. In a period of two years, 83 percent of all local government units nationwide had attended an orientation session on the new law and its implementing rules and regulations.[1] By 2005, the GPPB had prepared trainers from various ministries to carry on the mammoth task of training procurement officers countrywide so the new implementing rules and regulations could be put into effect for all government procurement operations. A timeline of activities undertaken after the law was passed in 2003 is shown in figure 7.1.

Ensuring Public Understanding of Reform

In August 2006, the GPPB organized a multistakeholder workshop that involved the GPPB staff; relevant government agencies; the Presidential Anti-Graft Commission; the Office of the Ombudsman; faith-based organizations, such as the Roman Catholic Bishops Conference of the Philippines; and business sector groups, including the Philippine Contractors Association and the National Citizens' Movement for Free Elections. The group of multistakeholders recognized that implementing procurement reform posed many challenges. There was little information shared systematically with coalitions that supported passage of the procurement law. One of the key conclusions of the multistakeholder workshop was that a comprehensive communication strategy had to be developed to increase understanding of new procurement processes and of various groups' roles in ensuring the successful implementation of procurement reform.

Figure 7.1. Implementation Timeline: Procurement Reform in the Philippines, 2003–08

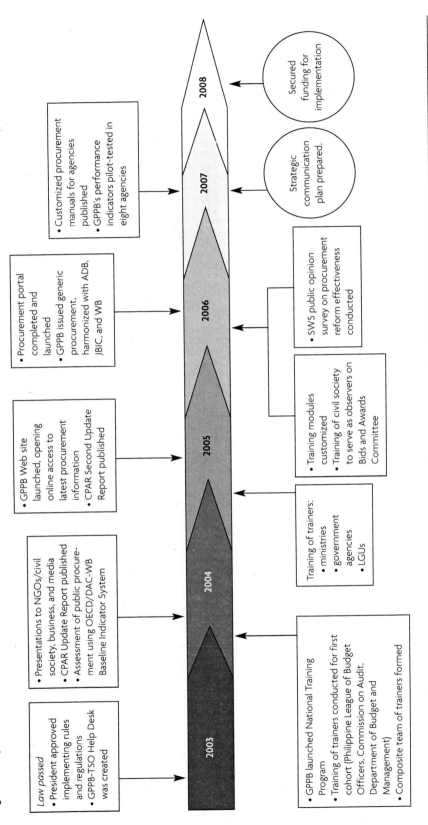

Sources: Authors' illustration, with input from Cecilia D. Vales, based on results of discussions held among reform agents from government, civil society, and the private sector at a communication planning workshop. Manila, August 2006.

Note: ADB = Asian Development Bank; CPAR = Country Procurement Assessment Report; GPPB-TSO = Government Procurement Policy Board Technical Support Office; JBIC = Japan Bank for International Cooperation; NGO = nongovernmental organization; OECD/DAC = Organisation for Economic Co-operation and Development/Development Assistance Committee; SWS = Social Weather Stations; WB = World Bank.

Left unanswered was the question, What did people know about procurement law and its intended impact on their lives? In November 2006, the Social Weather Stations research institution conducted a national survey. Its key result was not surprising, but it was troubling because it highlighted the need for government to step up its communication efforts and to reach out to the general public and to its coalition of supporters to sustain public interest and momentum during reform implementation. The survey (Social Weather Stations 2006) revealed the following findings (which are illustrated in figures 7.2 through 7.5):

- Only 13 percent of a nationally representative sample of 1,200 respondents were aware of the new Procurement Reform Law, although a majority believed that such a law would help reduce corruption in government contracts (p. 9).
- About one third of respondents believed that public officers were more careful about the misuse of funds in government contracts (p. 20).
- There was strong public support for specific provisions of the law, with three quarters of respondents stating that specific provisions (such as publication of bidding notices, invitations to nongovernmental organizations to observe the process, bidding carried out in public, and electronic publication of winning bids on the procurement Web site) definitely were needed (p. 12).

Figure 7.2. Public Attitudes toward the Procurement Reform Law

Despite low public awareness of the law . . .

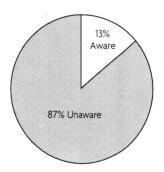

. . . the majority believes the law will help reduce corruption.

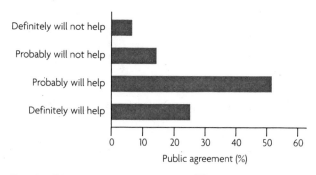

Question 105:

We have a law that provides for the standard rules in public bidding for government projects to guarantee that all contractors are given equal opportunity to join and win a government contract. This is called the Government Procurement Reform Act or RA9184. Have you heard or read something about it?

Question 106:

Do you think this law will help reduce corruption in government contracts?

Source: Public Opinion on Procurement Reforms, Social Weather Stations Survey, 2006.
Note: RA9184 = Republic Act No. 9184.

Figure 7.3. Public Support for Provisions of the Procurement Reform Law

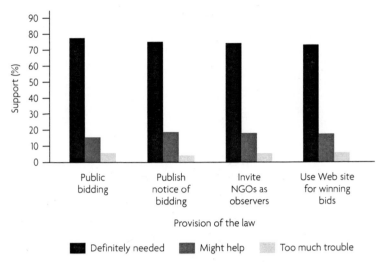

Source: Public Opinion on Procurement Reforms, Social Weather Stations Survey, 2006.
Note: NGO = nongovernmental organization.

Figure 7.4. Public Beliefs and Attitudes toward Corruption in Government Contracting

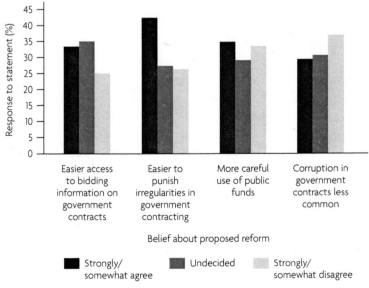

Question 88:

I have here some statements which may reflect how people feel or think about certain matters at present. Please tell me if you agree or disagree with these statements.

Source: Public Opinion on Procurement Reforms, Social Weather Stations Survey, 2006.

Figure 7.5. Public Willingness to Take Action in Support of Reform

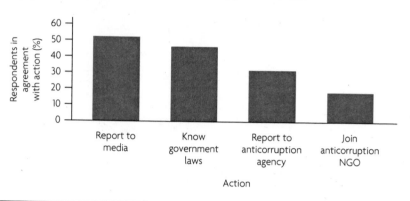

Source: Public Opinion on Procurement Reforms, Social Weather Stations Survey, 2006.
Note: NGO = nongovernmental organization.

- More than half of respondents stated they would report wrongdoing to the media to help reduce corruption in government contracts, and one third said they would alert a government anticorruption agency (p. 34).

Communication Challenges

The survey results provided the GPPB with key information about people's attitudes, perceptions, and motivations. Creating a comprehensive communication strategy demanded that other program elements be put in place so that messages would resonate with various audience segments and would trigger action among various constituencies.

Finding the Right Communication Expertise

Assessments done in the early years of implementation showed that the design of a comprehensive communication strategy should target both internal audiences (those people working in the public sector, including mid-level managers, bureaucrats, policy makers, and politicians at national and local levels) and external audiences (civil society, the media, and opponents of reform within various ministries and at national and local government levels). Behavior change goals are difficult to achieve because new practices and sweeping reform can run into opposition, and entrenched interests may block reform efforts. To target each of the audiences with effective messages passed along appropriate channels, it was necessary to put together the right mix of communication know-how.

Although the Philippines boasts of good communication expertise, finding the right mix of skills for the particular task at hand was difficult. A communication program to support implementation of the Procurement Reform Law required a specific blend of expertise to undertake various tasks: the client-driven orientation of specialists in social marketing, the instincts of political communicators in

Table 7.1. Decision Tool: Procurement Reform Law Implementation, Internal Communications

Management Objectives:

- To develop operational networks of interagency and cross-sectoral champions
- To equip agency and sectoral champions to implement the procurement reforms

Audience	Behaviors	Messages		Channels	Evaluation
		Takeaway Message	Supporting Data		
Top-level management (heads of procurement entity, secretaries, board directors)	• Implement the procurement reform law and its guidelines down to the lowest level of the agencies or LGUs and actively support GPPB initiatives • Appoint good and honest managers • Establish IAUs and make them operational, according to international standards	• "Public office is a public trust." • "Leave a legacy of a graft-free agency and a good reputation and track record." • "Good procurement practice will result in more funds for projects, and it is fundamental to building a strong and graft-free agency or LGU." • "Building links and sharing experiences with other agencies and other stakeholders (including CSOs, NGOs, and suppliers) make for good procurement." • "A good IAU will help me make timely and informed decisions." • "Procurement policies are practical and are intended to make life easier."	• Constitutional mandate (1987 Const., Art. 2, Sec. 1) • OMB/PAGC investigative reports • COA/internal audit findings • Public opinion surveys • National and international surveys	• Administrative issuances to support the law within the agency • Annual forum for the head of the procuring entity • Awards for best-performing agencies in procurement (Best BAC, Best CSO, and so forth) • Procurement newsletter as venue to announce programs	• Percentage of agencies complying with the law • Number of orders issued outlining the strategy for implementing the law • Percentage of IAUs established • Number of agencies/LGUs actively participating in the procurement reform network • Percentage of nationwide certified procurement professionals • Percentage of agencies having good APPI scores • Regular attendance of the members at GPPB meetings • Percentage of agencies with no unfavorable procurement findings by the COA • Percentage of agencies with no unfavorable procurement findings by CSOs through their reports

(continued on next page)

Table 7.1. Decision Tool: Procurement Reform Law Implementation, Internal Communications *(continued)*

Audience	Behaviors	Messages		Channels	Evaluation
		Takeaway Message	Supporting Data		
CSOs	• Appreciate relevance of procurement activities, vis-à-vis the organizations' stake in effective and transparent procurement as taxpayers • Consider themselves to be partners in promoting good governance • Submit observation reports to the head of the procuring entity and other oversight agencies; and consistently follow up the activities undertaken, particularly those concerning "red flags" and adverse findings • Actively participate as observers in the bidding process and in implementing the procurement reform law	• "Good procurement results in proper use of taxes." • "Reform results in improvements in the community." • "Take pride in providing a positive contribution to your community and your country." • "Transparent procurement prevents corruption."	• Studies about leaks • Annual reports on fund source and utilization • Testimonies of people who have experienced or perceived improvements • Data or surveys showing increased investments (local, national) resulting from good news • CSO reports • Corruption index and regular surveys on corruption	• Regular workshops and dialogues for CSOs within the alliance of NGOs and participating agencies • Regular workshops and dialogues with government agencies • Strengthened alliances among CSOs	• Increased presence of CSO observers at national and local biddings • Increased number of observers
Reformers in the media	• Publish good procurement practices/news and build on the success of the procurement reform network	• "Responsible journalism helps build confidence in valuable reform initiatives." • "Good news sells as much as bad news."	• Testimonies of people who have experienced or perceived improvements • Perception surveys or polls • Increased circulation of good news • Data or surveys showing increased investments (local, national) resulting from good news	• Orientation sessions • Face-to-face meetings with media groups, backed up by statistics and data on procurement • Regular procurement columns/features in national newspapers or radio/TV spots	• Increased number of reports on procurement (national and local, good and bad)

COA	• Harmonize audit tasks with reform initiatives • Understand and require implementation of the procurement reform law • Be more proactive in working with IAUs (the team approach) • Be more proactive in observing biddings	• "You are an important partner in the implementation of the procurement law."	• Cost of unliquidated cash advances related to questionable procurement • Percent of convictions based on COA audit reports	• Meetings to trigger issuances of support or cooperation, that is, appointment of champions	• Degree of variance between internal audit and external audit findings • Percentage of biddings with COA presence
Head of procuring entity	• Institutionalize good procurement practices in the agency or LGU • Sustain gains in procurement reforms within the agency or LGU • Resist external political pressures • Implement the procurement reform law and its guidelines in the agency or LGU • Support development of the cadre of procurement professionals within the agency	• "Good procurement practice is fundamental to building a strong and graft-free agency or LGU." • "Leave a legacy of a graft-free agency and a good track record." • "Savings in procurement will result in more funds for other worthwhile projects of the agency or LGU." • "Quality in procurement leads to better public service." • "Good procurement increases the confidence that IFIs and other agencies have in the procuring entity." • "Well-trained procurement personnel will result in more efficient procurement."	• APPI scores • COA/internal audit reports • Public opinion surveys • National and international surveys	• Administrative issuances to support training procurement personnel in procurement law • Annual forum for the head of the procurement entity • Awards for best-performing agencies in procurement (Best BAC, Best CSO, and so forth) • Procurement newsletter as venue to announce programs	• Favorable public opinion polls • Number of favorable media reports versus number of negative media reports • Positive assessments from IFIs • Percentage of agencies complying with the law • Number of orders issued outlining the strategy for implementing the law • Number of procurement personnel attending procurement workshops • Percentage of nationwide certified procurement professionals • Percentage of agencies having good APPI scores • Percentage of agencies with no unfavorable procurement findings by the COA • Percentage of agencies with no unfavorable procurement findings by CSOs through their reports

(continued on next page)

Table 7.1. Decision Tool: Procurement Reform Law Implementation, Internal Communications *(continued)*

| Audience | Behaviors | Messages | | Channels | Evaluation |
		Takeaway Message	Supporting Data		
BAC, BAC Secretariat, TWG, procurement office	• Act as champions for consistent and full implementation of procurement reforms • Study and consistently comply with the procurement reform law, rules, and procedures • Consider bidders to be strategic partners in the smooth procurement process • Be accountable for procurement successes and failures • Be zealous in the performance of their procurement functions • Act with proper decorum and in a professional manner at all times when dealing with bidders	• "We are vanguards of anticorruption, integrity, economy, and efficiency in procurement." • "We are experts in procurement." • "We take pride in a graft-free agency or LGU." • "We have the respect of all stakeholders." • "Good procurement is an indication of good performance." • "We take pride in our role as procurement professionals." • "We should have norms of conduct to follow as procurement personnel."	• APPI scores • COA/internal audit reports • Client satisfaction surveys • Public opinion surveys • Periodic reviews of improvements in the procurement process	• Achievement awards or recognition system for procurement excellence • Training and seminars on procurement rules, processes, and practices, as well as on values formation, team building, and proper decorum • Meetings and workshops on procurement • Newsletters • Information materials • Internet-based training or distance learning	• Positive monitoring and evaluation reports • Positive results in contractors' and suppliers' surveys • Positive assessments from IFIs • Percentage of nationwide certified procurement professionals • Percentage of agencies having good APPI scores • Percentage of BACs within the agencies with favorable COA procurement findings • Percentage of BACs with favorable procurement findings by CSOs through their reports • Percentage of BAC, BAC Secretariat, procurement units, and TWG attending regular trainings
Civil society organizations and professional associations	• Study procurement rules and procedures • Observe and consider the government's working environment • Fulfill the observer role adequately by recognizing and reporting "red flags" • View participation in the procurement reform as part of their mission for social transformation	• "Ensuring transparency in public procurement is part of the organization's mission against corruption." • "Good procurement results in proper use of taxes." • "Reform results in improvements in the community." • "Take pride in providing a positive contribution to your community and your country."	• Observation reports to management and the head of the agency or LGU • Agency performance reports by observers • Reports and complaints from professional associations' member-firms	• Achievement awards or recognition system for observers • Observers' reports to oversight agencies, the procuring entity, and their own organizations • Regular training programs for CSOs • Regular workshops and dialogues with government agencies • Continuing dialogues	• Increased presence of CSO observers at national and local biddings • Increased number of observer reports for management, OMB, and COA

Stakeholder	Actions	Messages	Data/documents	Activities	Performance indicators
	For professional associations: provide technical expertise and opinions on procurement processes and practices	"Help the government deliver basic services and save precious funds for more projects."			with other CSOs to recruit more observers
Technical experts (estimators, designers, specification writers, and bid document preparers)	Prepare designs, estimates, bid documents, and specifications conforming to acceptable standards and industry practice; Maintain the highest levels of professionalism and ethical standards in conformance with the procurement reform law, anticorruption laws, and professional codes	"We are experts in our field of work." "We are accountable for the accuracy and quality of designs and specifications." "We take pride in a graft-free agency or LGU." "We have the respect of all stakeholders."	Variance analyses; Estimates and budgets; Design and cost estimation reports	Preprocurement meetings; Dialogues and consultations with procurement and project implementation personnel; Quality assurance and value engineering, systems for design and cost estimation; Training and seminars on procurement rules, quality assurance and value engineering, systems for design and cost estimation; Newsletters	Success rate in procurement; Presence or absence of protests and litigation; Limited cost overruns and variation orders; Positive monitoring and evaluation reports; Positive results in contractors' and suppliers' surveys; Positive assessments from IFIs; Percentage of favorable COA procurement findings
Bidders	Study the procurement rules and processes; Comply with procurement rules and procedures with thoroughness and proper preparation; Desist from collusive and fraudulent practices; Avoid making nuisance protests; Submit responsive and competitive bids	"Good procurement makes for good business." "A transparent procurement process provides equal opportunity for all parties." "Good-quality service promotes a good reputation and more business." "Legitimate business practices promote credibility and competent governance."	Awarded projects; Track record; Public opinion surveys; Qualified bidders; BAC evaluation reports; Observation reports from COA and CSO observers; Contractors' performance evaluations; Increased financial returns and sales	Regular training programs for bidders; Regular dialogues and consultations with agencies; Prebid conferences; Face-to-face meetings with chambers of commerce and professional associations; Regular columns in business newspapers or radio/TV spots on procurement	Presence or absence of protests and litigation; Percentage of failed bids versus total number of bids; Percentage of satisfactory contractors/suppliers' performance evaluations versus total number of contracts; Increase in the number of qualified bidders for government

Source: Authors' compilation, based on communication planning workshop discussions held in Manila, August 2006.

Note: APPI = Agency Procurement Performance Indicator; BAC = Bids and Awards Committee; COA = Commission on Audit; CSO = civil society organization; GPPB = Government Procurement Policy Board; IAU = internal audit unit; IFI = international financial institution; LGU = local government unit; NGO = nongovernmental organization; OMB = Office of the Ombudsman; PAGC = Presidential Anti-Graft Commission; TWG = technical working group. The tool reflects circumstances as of August 24, 2006, based on results of discussions among participants from government agencies, donors, civil society organizations, media, and faith-based organizations during the Communication Strategy Development workshop held in Manila, Philippines, in August 2006.

mounting public advocacy campaigns, and the behavior change communication field experience of specialists based in nongovernmental organizations.

The internal communication strategy (table 7.1) addresses the stakeholder groups within the government structure who will be responsible for implementing the new procurement guidelines and external audiences (such as civil society) who have supported passage of the Procurement Reform Law. These groups are considered stakeholders relevant to an internal communication strategy because they have been active partners in the coalition that supported the passage of the law.

The external communication strategy (table 7.2) seeks to assist audiences outside the formal government structure (including donors, government employees' associations, and such external groups as the private sector and members of the media) who were not active partners in the earlier phase of securing passage of the Procurement Reform Law.

Whereas the internal communication strategy focuses on sustaining the interest and involvement of the pro-reform coalition, the external communication strategy aims to generate broad-based support for the successful implementation of the Procurement Reform Law.

Mobilizing Resources for Communication

Securing adequate support for communication programs has always been a challenge, particularly for reform programs. Prior to the passage of the Procurement Reform Law, donors were reluctant to finance communication activities that focused on the legislature for fear that the funded activities would be interpreted as an engagement in partisan politics. Nevertheless, some donors lent a hand to procurement reform, as allowed by their institutional mandates: The U.S. Agency for International Development (USAID) financed research that reviewed government procurement laws and their implementation over a number of years. The Asian Development Bank and the World Bank provided funds to build the capacity of a new civil society organization, Procurement Watch Inc., which played a central role in orchestrating the efforts of civil society groups to support passage of the procurement reform (Campos and Syquia 2006).

When the law was passed, donors monitored the progress of implementation in various ways. In partnership with the GPPB, the World Bank and others in the donor community—including the Asian Development Bank, USAID, the Japan Bank for International Cooperation, the Canadian International Development Agency, the Australian Aid Agency, and the European Commission— jointly prepared a series of Country Procurement Assessment Reports (CPARs). The 2002 report (World Bank 2003) highlighted the risks in the prevailing public procurement system that led to the passage of the omnibus Procurement Reform Law. By 2004–05, the CPAR (World Bank 2003, 2005) documented progress in improving the public procurement system, mainly in the increased

Table 7.2. Decision Tool: Procurement Reform Law Implementation, External Communications

Management Objective:

- To generate more public participation in the procurement process and in serving as watchdogs, to lessen corruption and manage government resources more efficiently

Audience	Behaviors	Messages		Channels	Evaluation
		Takeaway Message	Supporting Data		
National and local legislators (Senate, House, and *Sanggunian*) and the Office of the President	• Strongly support the implementation of procurement reforms • Improve transparency in procurement of PDAF projects	• "Supporting the procurement reform law as an anticorruption measure will help build public trust and confidence." • "Transparent procurement of PDAF projects builds my credibility with my constituents."	• Public opinion • Track record of good accomplishments • COA/internal audit reports • More visible projects	• Regular dialogues and consultations with national and local legislators • Regular reports on PDAF utilization, including publication in local and national newspapers • Radio/TV programs featuring successful PDAF projects	• Lower costs for congressional initiatives • Number of PDAF projects successfully implemented • Number of legislators supporting the implementation and enforcement of the procurement law
Government employees' associations	• Report to the proper authorities problems of corruption in their agencies • Detect "red flags" and be vigilant in procurement processes in the agencies and LGUs; and guard against deviations in the procurement process	• "Government employees play an important role in policy advocacy and implementation." • "Your vigilance will help improve good governance in your agency." • "Take pride in working for an agency that has a good reputation."	• Agency audit reports • Corruption survey of the agency • Lifestyle check of agency officials • Statements of assets and liabilities of agency officials	• Orientation of officials on the procurement law • Reports on procurement activities of the agency during general assemblies of the associations • Regular dialogues on procurement with BAC officials and other agencies • Newsletters	• Increased number of involved associations • Number of associations reporting on procurement irregularities
Oversight agencies (DOF, COA, NEDA, GPPB, DBM, OMB, PAGC, and DTI)	• Support the implementation of the procurement reform law within their scope of responsibility	• "A collaborative oversight effort will bring about effective procurement reforms and reduce corruption."	• Technical studies • COA/internal audit reports • Cases filed by the Ombudsman, Department of Justice, PAGC • Country procurement assessment reports • Public expenditure reviews	• Regular dialogues and consultations with the oversight agencies • Newsletters • Online monitoring and evaluation system • GPPB Web site • Philippine government e-procurement system	• Number of policy guidelines supporting the procurement reform by oversight agencies

(continued on next page)

Table 7.2. Decision Tool: Procurement Reform Law Implementation, External Communications *(continued)*

Audience	Behaviors	Messages		Channels	Evaluation
		Takeaway Message	Supporting Data		
• Print media (publishers, editors, columnists, and reporters) • Broadcast media (radio, TV owners, newsroom staff, researchers)	• Produce balanced, fair, and consistent reporting of procurement reforms	• "Fair reporting of procurement issues can generate wide interest among the public."	• Statistics from and case studies about success stories	• Meetings among the editors, owners, reporters, and researchers • Project observations	• Increased number of reports on procurement • Consistency of reporting on single issues
Civil society (church and religious groups, advocacy groups, professional associations, business groups, youth groups, senior citizens, academe, special interest groups, and labor groups)	• Integrate procurement reform in their evangelization program and be active in social concerns • Create an advocacy ministry/mission and provide people to serve as observers and project monitors • Create a funding system to support third-party observers and project monitors	• "Be involved in eradicating corruption." • "Know where your taxes are spent." • "Be vigilant in government procurement implementation."	• Budget utilization reports • Success stories • CSO reports	• Publication of budget utilization reports • Regular dialogues with GPPB and government agencies • Procurement features/columns in newspapers and in radio/TV spots • Published CSO reports • Published success stories	• Increased presence of CSO observers • Increased funding support for observers
General public	• Adopt more positive attitudes toward public procurement reforms • Increase trust in the government's efforts to increase the transparency of the procurement processes • Involve youth and elderly people in monitoring procurement activities • Continuously express their opinions • Volunteer as watchdogs	• "Better governance means better services." • "Transparent transactions lead to an informed public." • "Efficient use of resources and delivery of services lead to higher standards of living."	• Public opinion surveys • Lifestyle check reports	• Features/columns in newspapers • Radio/TV spots • Advertising campaign • Electronic media • Public forums • Public support from high-profile officials	• Favorable public opinion polls

| Donors, IFIs, and creditors | • Adopt the good anticorruption features of the procurement law
• Trust the BAC as a good estimate
• Increase the national competitive bid threshold | • "Supporting the government's procurement reform initiatives will make collusion and rigged biddings a high-risk/low-reward option." | • Comparison of prices between locally funded and foreign-funded projects
• Approved budgets for contracts and cost estimates | • Studies
• Reports comparing engineers' estimates with the trends for the approved budgets for contracts
• Focus group discussions
• PDAF
• Working groups | • Contract prices of IFI-funded projects are equal to or less than the approved budgets for government contracts
• Increased number of qualified bidders competing |

Source: Authors' compilation, based on communication planning workshop discussions held in Manila, August 2006.

Note: BAC = Bids and Awards Committee; COA = Commission on Audit; CSO = civil society organization; DBM = Department of Budget and Management; DOF = Department of Finance; DTI = Department of Trade and Industry; GPPB = Government Procurement Policy Board; IFI = international financial institution; LGU = local government unit; NEDA = National Economic Development Authority; OMB = Office of the Ombudsman; PAGC = Presidential Anti-Graft Commission; PDAF = Philippine Development Assistance Forum (a consultative group composed of donor agency representatives working with the Philippine government to identify development aid priorities). The tool reflects circumstances as of August 24, 2006, based on results of discussions among participants from government agencies, donors, civil society organizations, media, and faith-based organizations during the Communication Strategy Development workshop held in Manila, Philippines, in August 2006.

use of national competitive bidding thresholds and prior reviews. By 2006, a CPAR mission began to show concern about the pace and scope of reform implementation. The mission revisited key issues: improvement of monitoring tools to measure the reform's impact at the national and local government levels, strengthening of the communication strategy to support reform implementation, and ensuring active participation of civil society and the private sector.

Managing the Risk of Opposition and Vested Interests

Pockets of opposition and the exercise of indiscretion among powerful and influential elites threatened the successful implementation of procurement reform. These vested interests expressed their concerns to legislative and executive officials. Reports surfaced about a foreign company's proposal believed to be in violation of the national procurement rules—a proposal suggesting that government invest in a national broadband network for public offices. A newspaper article ("Good Law, Corrupt Officials") published in October 2007 reported that Benjamin Diokno, secretary of budget and management, made an impassioned plea during a Senate meeting to urge senators to protect the procurement law, which he described as "world class," from being emasculated by vested interests.

As the limits of the law continue to be tested, and implementation of the procurement law proceeds as a work in progress, the dedicated leadership of reform implementers and a committed coalition of allies has become the key factor in ensuring eventual success in the Philippines' reform process.

Note

1. Cecilia Vales, lead procurement officer in the World Bank Philippines Country Office, provided information on the key procurement reform milestones during the implementation period, 2003–07.

References

Campos, J. Edgardo, and Jose Luis Syquia. 2006. *Managing the Politics of Reform: Overhauling the Legal Infrastructure of Public Procurement in the Philippines.* World Bank Working Paper 70. Washington, DC: World Bank.

Social Weather Stations. 2006. "Public Opinion on Procurement Reforms." Manila, Philippines.

World Bank. 2003. *Philippines: Country Procurement Assessment Report.* Report 26378. Washington, DC: World Bank.

———. 2004. *Philippines Country Procurement Assessment Report, Update.* Report 30221. Washington, DC: World Bank.

———. 2005. *Philippines: Country Procurement Assessment Report, 2nd Update.* Report 40333. Washington, DC: World Bank.

8

The West African
Gas Pipeline Project

In 2001, the World Bank approved a Regional Integration Assistance Strategy for West Africa. This strategy was prepared in response to requests from the governments and regional organizations of West Africa, where regional integration is a recurring theme in most political and economic debates.[1]

Building on West Africa's own approach to regional integration, the Bank's assistance strategy was designed to create a more unified and open regional economic space to promote deep market integration for goods and services throughout the region. This integration would spur regional producers to become more competitive and would prompt better integration into the global market. If both of those things were to occur, the Bank's ultimate objective of accelerating growth and reducing poverty in West Africa likely would be achieved.

Four principles guided the design of the World Bank's assistance strategy: (1) respect for the subsidiarity and coherence of national programs; (2) focus on the private sector and civil society as the main engine of integration, as participants in the design and implementation of policies, and as the primary stakeholders and beneficiaries of integration; (3) emphasis on pragmatism and progressiveness in making regional integration schemes operational, recognizing the institutional and political capacity of countries; and (4) pursuit of partnerships to harmonize efforts among donors and to gain optimal benefits from the endeavor.

The West African Gas Pipeline (WAGP) Project, started in 2004 and just completed in 2009, has been one of the World Bank's major operations in fostering regional economic and political integration to achieve accelerated growth. It involved harnessing abundant and cheap natural gas from Nigeria to replace expensive alternative fuels consumed by the power, industrial, mining, and commercial sectors in Benin, Ghana, and Togo.

Nigeria is a resource-rich country with a total of 148 million people, the largest population in Africa. Its major income source is the oil industry, which provides about 95 percent of Nigeria's foreign exchange earnings and more than 80 percent of its GDP. As the sixth-largest oil producer in the world and the fifth-largest producer among members of the Organization of the Petroleum Exporting Countries, it has earned approximately $300 billion in oil royalties over the last four decades. Nigeria has the seventh-largest gas reserves in the world—double its oil reserves in energy terms.[2]

A sound political environment produced by the successful transition from a dictatorial regime to an open democracy in 1995 and by strong and effective national leadership spurred the country's progress toward macroeconomic stability. Its economy grew from an average of approximately 2.0 percent between 1995 and 1999 to an estimated 5.6 percent between 2000 and 2007.[3] In addition, the government demonstrated its commitment to improve governance by its participation in and full implementation of the Extractive Industries Transparency Initiative. Launched in September 2002, the initiative promotes transparency in oil and gas revenues by making public the amounts of money that extractive companies pay to the government in fees and taxes and the amounts of money the government receives from those companies.[4]

Benin, with a relatively small population of 8.8 million in 2006,[5] achieved significant progress in sustaining economic growth following economic and political crises in 1989. The government was successful in implementing a structural adjustment program that helped establish fiscal discipline, an open economy, and a favorable private sector environment. Despite these achievements, however, Benin still faces significant economic and social vulnerabilities arising from limited competitiveness and a cotton-dependent economy, weak institutional and administrative capacity, high population growth, gender inequities, and the prevalence of HIV/AIDS.

Like Nigeria, Ghana completed a smooth political transition to a democratic government and has had three democratically elected governments during the last 15 years, the latest in 2009. A favorable political climate, sound macroeconomic policies, and effective monetary and fiscal management led to impressive economic performance and sustained growth, with real GDP growth rising to 6.3 percent in 2007 (from 4.5 percent in 2002). Social indicators also improved. With a population of 23.5 million in 2007, the country has benefited from increased private sector investments in the cement, mining, and agro-processing industries. Growth in the service sector in tourism, banking, and communications also has increased during the last decade. And income from foreign remittances provided by the increasing number of Ghanaian professionals, estimated at $780 million in 2003, further has boosted the country's positive growth. GDP annual growth averaged 6.4 percent in 2006–07.[6]

Togo experiences continued volatile political and economic circumstances, following strong economic performance from 1960 to the mid-1970s (when real GDP annual growth rates averaged 7 percent). With a population of 6.5 million in 2007, Togo had an agriculture-dependent economy that provided 40 percent of the country's GDP and employed 75 percent of the labor force. Cotton, coffee, and cocoa exports contributed about 35 percent of total export earnings. Phosphate mining, its most important industrial activity, generated about 28 percent of exports n 2007.[7]

Political uncertainty hampered Togo's ability to reverse its economic decline. Government economic reform efforts launched in the late 1980s failed to take off, and subsequently they led to a 22 percent fall in GDP over the next decade. Beginning in mid-1998, the weak macroeconomic situation worsened because of a precarious political situation, declining cotton prices, and persistent problems in phosphate production. In 2001, Togo enjoyed a slight economic recovery, posting a real GDP growth rate of 2.7 percent rising to 3.9 percent in 2006,[8] largely as a result of improved agricultural performance and a higher international market price for cocoa. However, the overall macroeconomic picture remained bleak in a weak fiscal environment and under continued political uncertainty that greatly discouraged private sector investment. The country incurred arrears to the World Bank, resulting in the suspension of lending operations.

Key Development Issues

Since the late 1990s Benin, Ghana, and Togo have faced increasing difficulties in meeting the growing demand for reliable and affordable electricity. In Ghana, annual electricity consumption rose an average of 8 percent over the period and placed an enormous strain on the country's state-owned utilities. To prevent a power supply crisis, the government took steps to diversify and build new supply sources (such as providing oil- and gas-fired generation plants to supplement hydro generation, which had been the only provider of power supply in the country), and it pursued reforms in the electricity sector to promote private investment and improve service provision. In Benin and Togo, major challenges in the sector included (1) a shortage of generation capacity to meet increasing electricity demand in Benin, (2) high dependence on imports through a single interconnection with Ghana, (3) high operating costs and poor-quality service in the northern regions of Benin and Togo, and (4) the low level of electricity penetration in urban and rural areas.

Environmental and social issues in the oil and gas sector also presented serious development concerns. The Niger Delta in Nigeria, a major source of the country's oil wealth and a major source of oil exports to other West African countries, is one of the poorest areas in the country. High population density and deteriorating social and economic conditions have increased the vulnerability of the poor in the Delta. The high incidence of water-related illnesses, limited supply of potable water, depletion of valuable land as a result of riverbank erosion, declining fisheries and agricultural productivity, and limited income-earning opportunities are among the main concerns. Also, oil companies' differential treatment of communities that did and did not produce oil[9] engendered social inequities and fragmentation and roused the Delta's deep-seated interethnic conflicts that began with the trading of slaves and palm oil. These conflicts almost blossomed into open armed rebellion in the area in late 2007.

Project Profile

The World Bank's $590 million assistance for the WAGP Project was a joint undertaking of Benin, Ghana, Nigeria, and Togo. In January 2003, the four states signed a treaty on the project, and in May they signed the International Project Agreement. These agreements established harmonized legal and fiscal regimes for the project in the states; and set the principles for the development, ownership, and operation of the WAGP.

The project included construction of 678 kilometers of pipeline that would transport natural gas from Nigeria to Benin, Ghana, and Togo through major spur lines. Ghana likely would buy more than 90 percent of the gas, which would be used mainly for power generation. Existing oil-fired plants would be converted and new gas turbine plants would be constructed. The other project components to be completed were (1) contracts to purchase natural gas from the producers; (2) agreements for the transportation of natural gas by the transporters; (3) agreements for the sale of foundation amounts of natural gas to the Benin Electricity Company and to Ghana's Volta River Authority (VRA)[10]; and (4) contracts for the design, engineering, construction, ownership, operation and maintenance, oversight, and political risk mitigation of the new pipeline.

Envisioned to provide affordable, efficient, and environmentally safe fuel to consuming countries, the project was expected to reduce energy supply costs and improve the reliability of energy systems in Benin, Ghana, and Togo, and to help reduce gas flaring.

Three entities were responsible for implementing the project: N-Gas Limited contracted for the purchase and sale of natural gas. The Nigeria Gas Company agreed to transport natural gas from the Niger Delta to a terminal near Lagos over the existing pipeline system. The West African Gas Pipeline Company (WAPCo), a newly formed entity, would build, own, operate, and transport natural gas over a new pipeline from the Lagos terminal to the offshore pipeline and then to spur lines in specific distribution areas.[11]

In addition to the International Project Agreement signed in May 2003, principal project agreements defined the operational responsibilities and the allocation of risks assumed by the parties involved. The private sector parties assumed the construction- and operations-related risks; and the public sector took on the payment risks under the foundation customer gas supply agreements, which were on a take-or-pay basis in U.S. dollars.[12] Political risk guarantees were provided by the International Development Association, the Multilateral Investment Guarantee Agency, and Zurich Overseas Private Investment Corporation to cover any payment defaults or breaches of contract.

Obstacles and Opportunities

The West African Gas Pipeline Project, with its scale and complexity, presented vast opportunities for development as well as major implementation challenges. To offset the damaging effects of anticipated risks, the project undertook effective mitigation measures. Doing so required addressing economic, financial, operational, political, and social risks that could delay successful preparation and completion of the project. The design and implementation incorporated key components to ensure strong compliance with social safeguard policies and prevent undue harm to people. Environmental impact assessments established the severity of potential negative impacts and the measures planned to mitigate them. (It should be noted, however, that conversion of oil-fired power plants to gas-fired plants will reduce overall carbon dioxide emissions by more than 100 million tones over a 20-year period.) Involuntary resettlement, supported by resettlement action plans, provided for proper public consultations with members of households who were being displaced by land acquisition and for fair compensation of their asset and income losses. Regular consultations and disclosures were undertaken to inform and engage stakeholders and special interest groups.

Issues raised in the consultations and risk analysis included waste generation and potential hazardous material spills, negative environmental and social impacts, the loss of economic livelihood of affected communities, and some potential cultural issues. The project also raised the public's attention to broader sociopolitical issues unresolved in the Niger Delta. Local nongovernmental organizations (NGOs) and interest groups used the project as a vehicle again to raise controversy over human rights and benefits issues in the Niger Delta (where there have been long-standing conflicts between Delta communities and the international oil companies) and over the World Bank's involvement in extractive industries.

Figure 8.1 presents the project's timeline and the major issues assessed during the project cycle. The issues are illustrated in the order in which they appeared. The top part above the center horizontal line outlines what were mostly risks for the company and the government. Below the center horizontal line are those that fell mainly on the World Bank. Issues enclosed in shaded ovals were major risks that needed extensive mitigation. The figure illustrates the different po-

Figure 8.1. WAGP Project Cycle and Risk Mitigation Measures

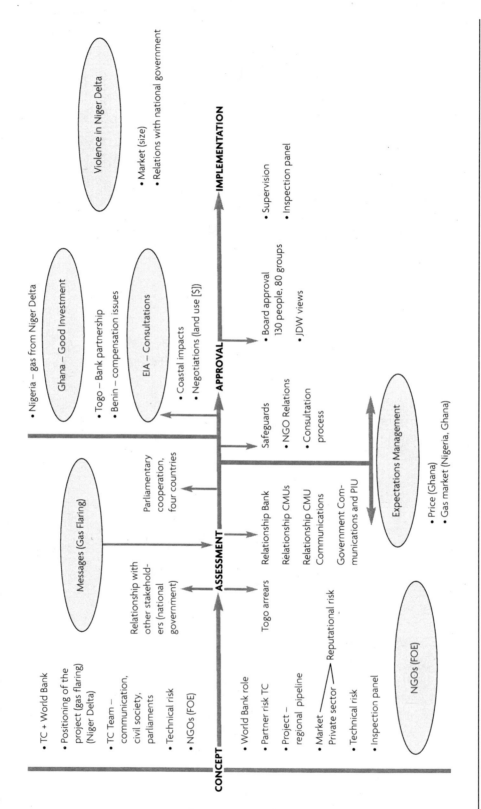

Source: Paul Mitchell, 2008.
Note: CMU = Country Management Unit; EIA = environmental impact assessment; FOE = Friends of the Earth; JDW = James D. Wolfensohn; NGO = nongovernmental organization; PIU = Project Implementation Unit; TC = Texaco Chevron; WAGP = West African Gas Pipeline.

litical, social, and cultural risks that arose during the project cycle. It also illustrates the need for continuous assessment as different risks appear at different times during the cycle.

Role of Strategic Communication

Key lessons from the World Bank's experience in similar energy and infrastructure operations have stressed the importance of undertaking a communication risk analysis and then using consultations and communication in building credibility, consensus, commitment to reform, and risk mitigation. Extensive consultations and the design and implementation of a communication strategy were crucial interventions identified in the project appraisal document (box 8.1).

The opportunity to undertake communication planning in the early stage of project design facilitates the systematic integration of a two-way communication process involving both upstream and downstream activities to build country ownership. Given that the project also involved four countries, the risk complexities were multiplied. Project planners involved in the West African Gas Pipeline Project used a well-designed communication strategy to understand how stakeholders viewed the project, identify the sociopolitical risks, manage expectations, assess capacity constraints, and build consensus about and commitment to the pipeline project. The decision tool for the communication strategy is presented in table 8.1.

Understanding Stakeholder Views through
Extensive Consultations

Stakeholder consultations began early in the project's conceptual design stage in 2000 and continued until 2004 when environmental agencies in all four

---

Box 8.1. Adequate Information/Communication and Consultations

To ensure sustainable implementation of a regional project in a sensitive infrastructure area, it is crucial to have a strong political and reputational risk assessment undertaken and to develop and implement a corresponding communications and consultations program to mitigate the potential risks and build country ownership.

This program of communications and consultations should take place prior to and during project design and implementation with beneficiaries and stakeholders the understandings reached between the groups should be formalized. This risk assessment was undertaken by the Bank and extensive consultations and communication work has been carried out and continue in the context of the Environmental Management Plans (EMPs) and a comprehensive communications strategy will be implemented by WAPCo and the WAGP Authority.

Source: World Bank 2004.

Table 8.1. Decision Tool: West African Gas Pipeline Project

Management Objective:
- To build ownership and public consensus for the project through effective consultation and active communication

Audience	Behaviors	Messages		Channels	Evaluation
		Takeaway Message	Supporting Data		
West African Gas Pipeline Company Limited	• Mount effective public information campaign to raise awareness and educate the public on the benefits of the project • Conduct open and regular dialogue with major stakeholders	• "A two-way communication process is necessary to enhance public understanding of the project's benefits, risk mitigation measures, and social assistance programs." • "Country ownership and public support can be achieved only through a participatory process and productive dialogue with key stakeholders, especially affected communities."	• Technical studies	• Meetings and consultations • Workshops and seminars	• Focus group
National government (ministries of energy and information, and related agencies)	• Disclose project plans and results of diagnostic and technical studies, properly and in a timely manner • Commit to improving institutional capacity for sustained communication efforts	• "To ensure broad public consensus, the government needs to build trust and credibility through adequate information exchange and sustained two-way communication with key stakeholders." • "Communication is not a one-time task or event. Sustained communication is necessary to maintain continued public consensus for the project."	• Consultation reports	• Information-sharing workshops • Public hearings • Stakeholder consultations	• Public opinion polls • Focus group • Evaluation survey
Parliament	• Support the project through legislative action and enactment of necessary laws	• "Parliament is a key partner and equally accountable for the success of the project. Timely action in legislative approvals and the enactment of laws will prevent delays in project implementation." • "Parliamentarians should listen actively to their constituents' concerns about the project's potential risks. They should help in educating the public about the benefits of the project." • "The private sector will benefit greatly from the project. We will engage actively in open dialogue with government and civil society."	• Interviews and consultations	• Parliamentary committee meetings	• Discussions resulting in parliamentarian support for legislative action; enactment of laws

| Civil society:
 • private investors
 • local and international NGOs
 • media
 • affected communities | • Provide affected communities information regularly about the environmental, social, and economic impacts of the project
 • Broaden avenues for enhanced civil society participation
 • Support the government's information and communication efforts through balanced reporting
 • Participate actively in public consultations
 • Assist in public information and education efforts, especially among less-informed communities | • "NGOs play a complementary role in bringing about active civic engagement. We can help enhance communication through civil society projects and activities."
 • "A proactive media is necessary to support the government's information and communication campaign. The media is a key partner; and is responsible for providing the public with complete, timely, and unbiased information about the project."
 • "We recognize the benefits of the project and trust that the government will ensure that displaced communities receive fair and just compensation." | • Technical and market studies
 • Stakeholder consultations
 • Beneficiary assessments
 • Interviews with influencers considered credible by various stakeholders | • Stakeholder consultations
 • Business roundtable meetings
 • Conferences and public development forums
 • TV, radio programs
 • Print media
 • Advertising campaign (streamers, posters, stickers, and giveaways) | • Stakeholder consultations
 • Media monitoring |

Source: Authors' compilation.

Note: NGO = nongovernmental organization.

countries held public hearings as part of the national review and clearance process.[13] WAPCo and the project team conducted more than 400 consultations in Benin, Ghana, Nigeria, and Togo, and they continued the dialogue undertaken during the construction and operational phases. The stakeholder groups consulted included the following:

- local communities, including fishermen and farmers, land owners, chiefs and traditional leaders, traditional councils, youth groups, and local authorities within the project corridor
- civil society organizations, such as the NGOs, community-based organizations, the mass media and journalists, National Canoe Fishermen Associations, and university faculty members
- government ministries, departments, and agencies; and regulatory and permitting authorities
- Cabinet ministers, Parliament energy subcommittees, individual parliamentarians, and the Economic Community of West African States Secretariat
- the business community, including foundation customers, trade and industry associations, the Council for Scientific and Industrial Research, and the Institution of Engineers
- media houses, organizations, and journalists who cover energy and environment issues.

Valuable insights about stakeholder perceptions and expectations were gathered from the various consultations in each country (table 8.2). Among the most important issues that emerged were ones pertaining to public safety and potential gas pipeline hazards (explosion, fire, and leaking), environmental impact assessment procedures, land acquisition and compensation procedures, and awareness raising and education about natural gas and the transmission pipeline. Other concerns pertained to community benefits and development assistance, the project's impact on fishing activities and beach erosion, access to electricity, reduction in electricity tariffs, local employment opportunities, and how the relationships between the pipeline project and the Niger Delta communities might affect supply reliability and continuity.

Identifying Sociopolitical Risks and Managing Public Expectations

Given the various concerns of key stakeholders about the project's possible negative impacts, the project team needed to gain a deeper understanding of the project's sociopolitical risks and to help define effective communications approaches to support risk mitigation measures. Sociopolitical risks are inherent in any large and ambitious development undertaking, and all the more so in a cross-border infrastructure operation such as the pipeline project. The 2004 political and reputational risk assessment carried out by the World Bank's Development Communication Team provided an in-depth diagnosis of social, political, and institutional issues that could affect country ownership and impede project preparation and implementation. The assessment mapped current and potential sources of influence across various sectors of society.

Focus groups and extensive consultations were held with key representatives of 70 organizations in the four countries. Active dialogues with the media, NGOs, and civil society representatives were undertaken to assess their perceptions of the project's risks and the necessary measures to protect the safety and interests of displaced communities. The assessment revealed strong political support for the project, and showed that stakeholder groups recognized its significant socioeconomic and environmental benefits. In Benin, stakeholders viewed the project as an important development initiative and stressed the need to address their major concerns about safety and adverse environmental im-

Table 8.2. Issues, Perceptions, and Expectations: Views from Stakeholders

Country	Major Stakeholders Consulted	Stakeholders' Key Issues and Concerns	Stakeholders' Perceptions, Attitudes, and Expectations
Benin	• Community • Government agencies • International organizations and NGOs • Business and media	• Land acquisition and compensation • Community benefits and employment • Need for support and participation • Permitting and regulations	• Value environmental benefits above all • Expect direct negotiations of compensation without any intermediary • Wish to be relocated within their communities

Ghana	• Government agencies
	• International organizations and NGOs
	• Business
	• Community
	• Media
	• National experts and educational institutions
		• Environmental issues and environmental assessment process
		• Permitting and regulations
		• Safety
		• Fish ecology
		• Land acquisition and compensation
		• Information exchange
			• Are enthusiastic about project benefits, particularly
			  • increase in country's industrial output through steady and cheaper energy supply
			  • improvements in local economy
			  • employment impacts
			• Public expects that fair compensation will be provided

Nigeria	• Community • Government agencies • Business	• Land acquisition and compensation • Health and environmental hazards • Loss of fishing grounds • Negative impact on agriculture • Community benefits	• View the project's impact on community positively • Believe the greatest benefit will accrue to compensated owners of land or property • Believe that provision of social services and community programs will secure future livelihoods
Togo	• Community • Government agencies • International organizations and NGOs • Business • National experts and educational institutions	• Environmental issues and environmental assessment process • Land acquisition and compensation • Information exchange • Fish ecology	• Expect a positive impact on the industry sector • Believe the greatest benefit will accrue to compensated owners of land or property

Source: Mitchell and Santi 2004.
Note: NGO = nongovernmental organization.

pacts. Benin's minister of energy was a strong project advocate, and his efforts to build good relationships with Parliament and to reach out to village chiefs and local communities helped promote the project's positive image. In Ghana, the enthusiastic response of many focus group and consultation participants led to high expectations of prompt and speedy project implementation. Within the Ghanaian legislature, the project had widespread support. In Nigeria, broad political consensus was noted, although parliamentary committees expressed concern about their limited involvement in the project and sought more active engagement in the process. In Togo, political leaders welcomed the project. With the country in arrears to the World Bank and lending operations suspended, however, a means of arranging financial assistance had to be found.

Although there was clear appreciation for the benefits of the project, stakeholder feedback indicated varying degrees of public expectations. For example, the assessment confirmed the high expectation that there would be employment opportunities and compensation, especially among affected communities, and general hope that pipeline construction would mean more employment in the four countries. It also revealed unrealistic expectations of substantial compensation for each square meter of land acquired for the project, an issue that particularly had to be addressed in Benin. Among the general population, expectations were high that the pipeline would prompt a significant reduction in the cost of residential energy.

Feedback received from various stakeholders interviewed for the assessment echoed many of the issues that had been raised in earlier consultations, but it also called attention to other significant issues that increased the risk of project failure if not properly addressed. These additional issues included (1) the project's financial viability and cost considerations, (2) the threat to safety arising from pipeline explosions, (3) WAPCo's likely failure to pay agreed prices for land and to meet its obligation to provide community services because of government involvement in the compensation process, (4) delays in land compensation and potential loss in escalation of land prices, (5) inequitable distribution of benefits within the general population and especially among communities directly affected by the pipeline, (6) longstanding social conflicts in Nigeria, (7) social instability in the Niger River Delta linked to violence in the region and the potential disruption of the gas supply, (8) the lack of government ownership and the private sector's possible takeover of the project, and (9) risks associated with poor communication and information flows between government and relevant organizations.

Assessing Capacity Constraints and Communication Challenges

Ensuring open, transparent, and reliable communication between and among key stakeholders was critical to building public consensus and sustaining commitment to change. An assessment of the communication environment revealed weak information flows between the executive branch and Parliament; between the government and NGOs; and among government, the media, and civil society groups. In all four countries, members of Parliament were concerned about the adequacy and timing of information received from the executive branch. In Benin, communication was weakest at the grassroots level. Affected communities received inadequate information from the local authorities and village chiefs. In Ghana, where the president gave a strong statement about the country's commitment to the project, members of Parliament were wary of the executive branch's exclusive handling of negotiations. Parliament's limited involvement in the process presented a potential risk. In Nigeria, too, poor communication between the executive and legislative branches was a problem. Parliamentary committees were especially concerned about having adequate and timely information needed to plan their legislative calendar effectively. In Togo, information flows were not balanced.[14] Most of the information disseminated focused on the technical aspects of the project rather than on the social concerns of the affected population. The general public had little knowledge about the project, although the media received adequate and timely information from WAPCo.

The lack of communication capacity led to poor communication flows. In Benin, the government's lackluster record of communication and the weak media effectively had disempowered the general public, limiting its access to information. In Ghana, difficulty in getting access to official documents concerning the project greatly dampened media interest, especially among the private and independent media. Some journalists used Web sites and NGOs as their primary sources of information about the project. In Togo, the Ministry of Energy held communication events but was not equipped to provide the extensive communication support needed for the project. The ministry was newly created and its organizational structure did not provide for a separate communications office. WAPCo undertook most of the communication efforts across all four countries, but it placed too much emphasis on the technical aspects of the project and did not adequately address the social impact on affected communities and the concerns of broader segments of the population.

Building Consensus and Commitment

The results of the communication assessment provided a solid framework for defining the scope and strategic focus of the project's communication strategy. The Development Communications Team from the World Bank's External Affairs Vice Presidency had recommendations that covered various aspects needed for an effective communication strategy: On the overall approach to communication, WAPCo needed to be more proactive, implementing a two-way communication process to support information sharing, active consultations, public education, and open dialogue. The clarity and consistency of messages from WAPCo were enormously important, as was the timely release of key project information. Regarding communication activities, a decentralized and country-driven approach was proposed to enable each of the four states to define country-specific, audience-focused communication tools and events. The team also emphasized such an approach to facilitate more active engagement with the media and Parliament and to promote stronger grassroots communication. Regular monitoring and evaluation of public events also was recommended to track the progress and effectiveness of the communication strategy.

Based on the assessment's recommendations and on further analysis, WAPCo designed a communication strategy aimed at (1) improving stakeholder outreach, (2) enhancing public understanding of the project's benefits and costs, (3) actively engaging legislators and supporting them in the timely passage of laws needed to implement the project, (4) improving working relationships with land administration agencies to ensure the just and timely compensation of affected households, and (5) soliciting stakeholder views on appropriate social capital programs for communities affected by the project. To achieve these objectives, WAPCo identified the following key result areas and objectives: (1) communication and image management; (2) government advocacy for agreements, permitting, and regulatory approvals; and (3) community engagement and stakeholder consultations. Among the high-priority activities defined to realize those objectives were developing the WAPCo identity, holding media orientations, producing communication materials, providing communication support for government activities and public hearings, monitoring and analyzing media reports, building knowledge about land acquisition and compensation procedures, enhancing support for the socioeconomic impact assessment, holding stakeholder consultations on the environmental impact assessment, supporting resettlement action plan activities and the social capital program for affected communities, and defining a policy on press releases and public inquiries.

Lessons Learned and Challenges Remaining

The project's broad-based consultations and its early and adequate focus on communication illustrate the positive impact of meaningful public participation in the project development process. In 2004, the World Bank's project appraisal mission confirmed the enthusiastic response and broad support for the West African Gas Pipeline Project, even among NGOs and interest groups concerned about the associated environmental and socioeconomic risks.

The process of consulting and communicating with all sectors of the population served as an in-depth diagnostic tool to gain a greater understanding of stakeholders' views, fears, and concerns, and as an advocacy tool on issues that warranted the attention of policy makers and legislators. Moreover, the emphasis on informed public participation helped achieve informed decision making in the project's planning and design stages. The communication process helped define the scope of public dialogue and the shape of critical mitigation measures to be addressed.

The WAGP Project experience underscored many of the key lessons learned in World Bank operations that have benefited from strategic communication:

- Consider communication in the planning stage of a project.
- Listen actively to stakeholders and maintain ongoing dialogue.
- Define the scope of public debate.
- Manage public expectations.
- Build consensus.
- Promote local ownership of a project.

Although outstanding public concerns about safety and adequate compensation remain even in 2009, when the first gas went through the pipeline into Ghana, the most critical challenge during the 2004–09 period has been to build adequate communication capacity within governments to sustain political support for the pipeline project. With the right institutional mechanisms in place, the West African Gas Pipeline Project achieved its declared mission objectives to make WAGP known, understood, and supported by all external constituents/stakeholders and to create the enabling environment that enables the key players to implement the project effectively.

Notes

1. Regional integration in West Africa primarily concerns 15 countries: Benin, Burkina Faso, Cape Verde, Côte d'Ivoire, The Gambia, Ghana, Guinea, Guinea-Bissau, Liberia, Mali, Niger, Nigeria, Senegal, Sierra Leone, and Togo. Those countries have a combined population of almost 300 million (2007 data) people, half of whom live in absolute poverty with an average per capita annual income just above $300.
2. Figures, accurate as of the end of 2007, are taken from the April 2009 *World Development Indicators* database.
3. Figures, accurate as of 2007, are taken from the April 2009 *World Development Indicators* database.
4. The initiative was launched by U.K. Prime Minister Tony Blair at the 2002 World Summit on Sustainable Development. As of June 2003, participants included the Nigerian National Petroleum Corporation, Chevron, Shell, and Total—the major oil companies operating in Nigeria.
5. Figures, accurate as of 2007, are taken from the April 2009 *World Development Indicators* database.
6. Figures, accurate as of 2007, are taken from the April 2009 *World Development Indicators* database.
7. Figures, accurate as of 2007, are taken from the April 2009 *World Development Indicators* database.
8. Figures, accurate as of 2007, are taken from the April 2009 *World Development Indicators* database.
9. Oil companies compensate oil-producing communities for environmental damage caused by oil exploration. The compensation usually takes the form of community programs, schools, hospitals, and cash. In the event of oil leaks, communities are given cash

compensation or local workers are hired to clean up the oil. Only 5 percent of the communities in the Niger Delta were oil-producing communities.

10. The Benin Electricity Company and the VRA are the foundation customers that underwrote the costs of the new pipeline.

11. WAPCo would be owned by an investment consortium of six companies with the following shares of ownership: ChevronTexaco West African Gas Pipeline Ltd. (36.7 percent), Nigerian National Petroleum Corporation (25.0 percent), Shell Overseas Holdings Ltd. (18.0 percent), VRA's Takoradi Power Company Ltd. (16.3 percent), Benin Gas Company (SoBeGaz) (2.0 percent), and Togo Gas Company (SoToGaz) (2.0 percent).

12. The public sector agreements included the Takoradi Gas Sales Agreement between VRA and N-Gas, which provided for the sale by N-Gas and the purchase by VRA of up to 120 million standard cubic feet of gas and defined the mode of payment and the liabilities in case of default; the Takoradi Gas Transportation Agreement between WAPCo and N-Gas covering the gas being sold by N-Gas under the Takoradi Gas Sales Agreement; the VRA Direct Agreement whereby N-Gas assigned to WAPCo the component of the VRA termination payment and arrears owed to N-Gas; and the Government Consent and Support Agreement, by which Ghana guaranteed to N-Gas and WAPCo the performance obligations of VRA under the Takoradi Gas Sales Agreement and the VRA Direct Agreement.

13. The Development Communications Team of the World Bank's External Affairs Vice Presidency organized consultation meetings that served as a forum for information sharing and stakeholder consultation. It also provided an opportunity for stakeholders to express their concerns about the project's environmental and socioeconomic impacts, and those concerns were considered in the environmental impact assessment process and the WAGP Project Environmental Plan.

14. Most of the energy correspondents interviewed during the assessment were not aware of public hearings held for the project.

References

Mitchell, P., and E. Santi. 2004. "Communication Needs Assessment, Back-to-Office Report." World Bank, Washington, DC.

World Bank. 2004. "The West African Gas Pipeline Project. Project Appraisal Document." Report AB493. World Bank, Washington, DC.